Daily Meditations (with Scripture)
for Busy Moms

by Patricia Robertson

ACTA Publications

Chicago, Illinois

Daily Meditations (with Scripture) for Busy Moms

by Patricia Robertson

Edited by Gregory F. Augustine Pierce
Cover Artwork by Abigail Pierce (age 4) and ISZ
Design and Typesetting by Garrison Productions

Special thanks to Helen Reichert Lambin, Suzette
Arsipe Lambin, and Rev. William Burke for help in
choosing the Scripture passages.

Copyright ©1993 by   ACTA Publications
                        4848 N. Clark Street
                        Chicago, Illinois 60640
                        312-271-1030

Library of Congress Catalog number: 93-072793

ISBN: 0-87946-085-7

Printed in the United States of America

Happy New Year

The world is silent as last night's revelers sleep. Only I am up to greet the dawn, myself and this nursing baby now asleep in my arms. I look out on the quiet new day and remember the promise of Christmas. The promise of Christmases gone by. The promise of this new child God has lent me to love.

Birds fly out over the fresh snow, leaving their footprints on the ground where they land. A squirrel jumps from branch to branch, knocking down snow. Already a new year has begun, leaving its small markings. Already a new life has begun, leaving her traces throughout our home.

Each year—each day—we mothers begin again. We vow to start over, to do better. And when we lie exhausted at night, ashamed of the many times we have failed to live up to our good intentions, we reassure ourselves with the promise that tomorrow—or next year—will be different. It's this promise of new beginnings that keeps us going.

Each morning brings a new day. Each January a new year. Each child a new chance to mother as God meant us to—in love with God and each other.

Then I saw a new heaven and a new earth. The former heaven and the former earth had passed away, and the sea was no more. Rv 21:1

Across the Kitchen Table

The kitchen table is the mother's workbench.

Important things can and will happen there—from early morning fights to late night discussions. From the mundane to the sublime.

Sometimes, when I am alone, I just sit at the kitchen table and stare. I sip my coffee and think . . . about the world, about my kids, about my husband, and about the wonder of it all.

Food from heaven you gave them in their hunger, /water from a rock you sent them in their thirst. Neh 9:15

The Good Mother

I once was under the illusion that such a creature as the "Good Mother" existed. The "Good Mother" stays home with her children. She bakes cookies and sews clothes. She is an immaculate housekeeper.

The "Good Mother" always has time for her children. She never even locks the bathroom door.

The "Good Mother" may work outside the home and put her kids in day care, but only as long as she feels sufficient guilt for doing so.

The "Good Mother" never raises her voice to her children or lets her kids aggravate her. And if they do, the "Good Mother" never lets them know.

She always cooks nutritious, healthy meals and serves them in such attractive ways that her family would never turn their noses up at them.

Illusions die hard.

———————————

When one finds a worthy wife, /her value is far beyond pearls. /She opens her mouth in wisdom, /and on her tongue is kindly counsel. /She watches the conduct of her household, /and eats not her food in idleness. /Her children rise and praise her; /her husband, too, extols her. Prv 31:10, 26-28

Evening Litany

Finish your snack. Put on your pajamas.

   Go to sleep.

Pick up your clothes. Get your milk.

   Go to sleep.

Brush your teeth. Read your book.

   Go to sleep.

Say your prayers. Climb in bed.

   Go to sleep.

No more stories. No more talk.

   Go to sleep.

No more water. Get back in bed.

   Go to sleep.

No more whispers. No more toys.

   Go . . . to . . . sleep.

Let my prayer be incense before you; /my
uplifted hands an evening sacrifice. Ps 141:2

Bargain-Hunting

I love a good deal. Somehow paying full price for something, even when I want it badly, is never as much fun as buying it on sale. There's something about paying full price that nags at me. I'm passing this obsession on to my children. They know how to get to me.

"Look, Mom, it's half-price. Can I get it?"

"Of course," I say. "How can we turn down such a bargain?"

But with God, there is no bargaining. The price is the same for everyone. It costs all of us—all our hearts, all our souls, and all our minds.

How do I teach my children what a bargain that is?

"You shall love the Lord, your God, with all your heart, with all your being, with all your strength, and with all your mind, and your neighbor as yourself." Lk 10:27

Dreamers

For years I've resisted my idealistic side. To me, being idealistic was the same as being naive, and I wanted none of that. Besides, the more idealistic a mother is the harder she falls when faced with the ugly realities of life.

But I've had to come to accept my idealism for my kids' sake. It's true that idealists set themselves up for big falls, but I'd rather my children fail than never try. I'd rather they be accused of naivete than give up on this world.

And so I have become an idealist. I want my children to be dreamers.

The star which they had seen at its rising preceded them, until it came and stopped over the place where the child was. They were overjoyed at seeing the star. Mt 2:9-10

Misplaced Anger

The boss yells at me and I come home and yell at my kids. Not for anything they actually did, but out of frustration, out of powerlessness. Everyone goes after those who are most vulnerable, and who is more so than our children? They are at our mercy, dependent on us for food, clothing, shelter and love. It appears safe to vent our feelings on them, for they can't retaliate . . . at least not right away.

Even the best of mothers have given in under the strain and taken out their misplaced anger on their children.

What is it that leads us to act that way? What terrible instincts lead us to act out against those who are helpless, whom we know—or at least believe—can't hurt us back? What law of self-preservation are we following when we do this? And how do we break the cycle?

_____

What I do, I do not understand. For I do not do what I want, but I do what I hate.
Rom 7:15

Picking Fights

My children's inexhaustible ability to pick fights with each other continuously amazes me. They fight over who sits where, what cups they drink out of, what clothes they wear and, when they've exhausted all of these possibilities, they fight for no reason I can discern.

Most days I just let them fight it out until one draws blood. Other days it gets to me, especially when I'm under a time bind such as getting them ready to go to school or church on Sunday. Then I find myself dragged into their fights as they find new energy to resist their common enemy—me.

Here in the desert the whole Israelite community grumbled against Moses and Aaron.
Ex 16:2

Paybacks

There are really no paybacks when it comes to mothering. We can never thank our own mothers sufficiently for what they gave us as children. Nor can they make up for what we didn't get or what bad things were done to us. The gap between mother and daughter never completely disappears. By the time we are mothers ourselves and understand some of what our mothers went through, they are grandmothers experiencing something totally different.

All that we can do is appreciate the good that our mothers did for us and try to do good for our own children in turn. We can't pay back the generation ahead of us, nor are we meant to, any more than our own children will be able to repay us. All we can do is do our best to raise our own children with love.

There is no greater gift we can give the generation of women before us.

If I, therefore, the master and teacher, have washed your feet, you ought to wash one another's feet. I have given you a model to follow, so that as I have done for you, you should also do. Jn 13:14-15

Calm before the Storm

I awaken, tired from having been disturbed twice during the night and not being able to get back to sleep. Still, I am calm. I have a busy day ahead of me, but I begin at peace.

Today will be different. There will be no early morning battles over what clothes to wear. I will firmly set limits and not lose it when those limits are repeatedly breached. There will be no running around the house at the last minute saying "Hurry, hurry, we're late." Everything will be done in its time. No last minute hunts for shoes. No fights about what to bring to day care or school. No arguments over the coats they'll wear or over taking their vitamins.

I am calm, in control, at peace.

Then, once again, chaos triumphs.

———————————————

You expected much; but it came to little; /and what you brought home, I blew away. Hg 1:9

The Mistress

I don't want to be your wife,

Your wife cooks and cleans.

She clips coupons and worries about bills.

She does the laundry, cleans the toilets

and looks out for your cholesterol.

I want to be your mistress,

To be swept away in a whirl of passion.

To be free of all responsibility

save to treasure your body—and you mine.

To make love till breath escapes us

and the world disappears.

Bring me, O king, to your chambers. Song 1:4

The Juggling Act

"There's only one of me and four of you, so you'll just have to wait," I tell my children as all of them come at me with demands. "I can only do one thing at a time."

My children don't accept this answer because they know I'm lying. They know that at any given moment I'm capable of doing at least two or three things. I'll have, for example, laundry going, supper in process, and dishes half done—all while answering several phone calls. No wonder they don't believe me.

Society rewards this ability to do more than one thing at a time. I'm told I'm efficient, a hard worker, that I really get the job done.

But I'm tired of this juggling act. The times that I give each of my children my undivided attention are few and far between. They are missing something . . . and so am I.

"Martha, Martha, you are anxious and worried about many things." Lk 10:41

Broken Dreams

"Mommy, do you still love us? Will you leave like Daddy?"

"Of course I love you, and your father does too. I'll never leave you."

The mother knows the answer to those questions, at least.

Because you are precious in my eyes /and glorious, and because I love you. Is 43:4

Let the Dance Begin

I watch my daughters dance, wondering, "when was the last time I felt such unbridled excitement?"

I bite my tongue and keep from telling my children to take it easy. They have yet to learn that sometimes the anticipation is more fun than the actual event itself. They have not yet experienced the hard realities of disappointment and disillusionment.

Amidst the responsibilities of motherhood, it's easy to lose the unreflective enthusiasm of youth.

Let the dance begin!

The prophetess Miriam, Aaron's sister, took a tambourine in her hand, while all the women went out after her with tambourines, dancing. Ex 15:20

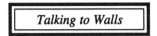

Talking to Walls

I talk to walls every day. Only in my case the walls have names—those of my children. I threaten, cajole, repeat myself for the thousandth time. Still nothing seems to penetrate those thick walls.

And then I wonder: If God is truly mother and father to me, am I as dense with God as my children are with me? Even while at prayer, I am more full of myself than attentive to God.

I talk to walls every day. Sometimes, miraculously, something I say sinks in. Maybe some things God says to me sink in.

Oh, that today you would hear his voice.
Ps 5:7

Catching God on the Run

Today's society is on the run. You grab a bite to eat, get coffee from your nearest take-out, and catnap between racing from one activity to another. As a mother I've often reassured myself with "Someday my life will be my own again." But then I am running from school play, to band practice, to football games, to dance recitals, to scout meetings, to the P.T.A., etc., etc., etc.

When I think about my days B.C. (before children) and remember the long hours of silent meditation or deep conversation with adult friends, I wonder if mothers are doomed to a life of spiritual mediocrity—a prayer life, at best, of spurts and starts, jumps and jolts.

But perhaps that's the prayer life best suited for today, an hour here, two minutes there, twenty minutes some other time . . . catching God on the run during those loose ends and in-between places in our lives.

With all prayer and supplication, pray at every opportunity in the Spirit. Eph 6:18

This Time

The news came today. The tests came back positive. This time will be different. This time she'll bring her baby to full term.

Still fears persist. She's afraid to think too much about it—afraid to get attached too soon to that precious life inside her.

She did not even have the chance to know the person she lost the last time. Yet it still hurts. Please, God, let her rejoice this time.

At dusk weeping comes for the night; /but at dawn there is rejoicing. Ps 30:6

It's Time

My mother is so ill, so old. Why doesn't God take her? She's lived out the portion of her days. So many have gone before, her parents, her husband, her son, one grandchild. She has more friends in the next world than in this one. It's time for her to join them.

My children don't like to hear me say these things. They want Grandma to live for them. They don't want her to go, don't want to hear me talk about her death. And yet talk I must.

I want Mom to be with Dad again. The day of his death is as real to me today as when it happened fifteen years ago. I see them together again and it comforts me. He is waiting for her. Let go, Mom, we will join you later.

Fear not death's decree for you; /remember, it embraces those before you, and those after. /This God has ordained for all flesh. Sir 41:3-4

The Quiet Child

What about the quiet child? The silent one, who never causes any trouble. Who quietly waits for any scrap that may come his way—any morsel of care and affection. Whose needs are just as great as those of the more vocal members of the family but go unmet because he remains silent?

What about the quiet children in our society? The homeless, the poor? Those who go to bed hungry, in tears? The victims of abuse in their own homes? How do we find those who suffer in silence?

What about the quiet children? How do we give them a voice?

_____

In just the same way, it is not the will of your heavenly Father that one of these little ones be lost. Mt 18:14

Far to Go

It will be different for my baby, this precious little girl. She won't have to face the same hardships I faced. I'll see to that. It'll be better for her than it was for her grandmother and me.

Sometimes I believe that, other times I don't. Sometimes it seems we've made no progress. Prejudice abounds. Sexism exists. Stereotypes still reign in people's hearts and minds. It's taken generations to get where we are today. Have we really come that far?

We've progressed and yet we haven't. There's still so far to go.

Will it be better for this next generation? I don't know. What I do know is that it will be different for my daughter.

May the children of your servants live on;
/may their descendents live in your presence.
Ps 102:29

People Pleasing

Beware the people pleaser. She'd sell her soul to smooth over conflict. Peace at all costs, she cries.

Even God doesn't ask such sacrifice from mothers, and yet we so often fall prey to this disease. We deny our needs, try to be whatever others want us to be.

We desire so much to be liked, to be loved, that we often end up alone because we have lost our very selves.

Beware the people pleaser.

Winnow not in every wind, /and start not off in every direction. /Be consistent in your thoughts; steadfast be your words. Sir 5:11-12

Perseverance

Kids know that if they pester Mom enough, eventually they will wear her down and get what they want. Mom gives in out of sheer frustration and tiredness, because it takes energy to keep saying no.

We can't wear God down, because God is limitless energy. Still, God often gives us our way.

Isn't that amazing?

And he said to them, "Suppose one of you has a friend to whom he goes at midnight and says, 'Friend, lend me three loaves of bread, for a friend of mine has arrived at my house from a journey and I have nothing to offer him,' and he says in reply from within, 'Do not bother me; the door has already been locked and my children and I are already in bed. I cannot get up to give you anything.' I tell you, if he does not get up to give him the loaves because of their friendship, he will get up to give him whatever he needs because of his persistence." Lk 11:5-8

> *Precious Moments*

My children have a *Precious Moments* Bible. It was given to them when they were infants and now sits in our living room on a table. I look at it and realize how apt the title is.

How precious are those moments I can sit quietly with scripture and allow God's word to feed me and strengthen me.

How precious are those moments when I realize that, however strangely and mysteriously, God is present with me.

How precious are those moments when I realize how special is each moment I have with my children.

I commend you to God and to that gracious word of his that can build you up and give you the inheritance among all who are consecrated.
Acts 20:32

Starving Children

"Eat your food. After all, there are children starving in Africa."

An old cliche, and yet there is a connection between the food we waste here and starving children elsewhere. Hard to grasp? It's hard enough for us adults to understand, much less our children.

But the connection remains. Those terrifying images of large eyed, swollen belly babies in Africa are more than pictures. They are a reality that our consumer society helps create.

I am not poor. My children are not starving. We can certainly afford to waste a little food now and then . . . or can we?

Agabus stood up and predicted by the Spirit that there would be a severe famine all over the world, and it happened under Claudius. So the disciples determined that, according to ability, each should send relief to the brothers who lived in Judea. Acts 11:28-29

Illusion

Oh, for a child who is just like me. Wasn't I the picture of obedience? Didn't I jump joyfully at the sound of my mother's first call. I never told her, "just a minute, just let me finish reading this paragraph or watching this show," and then go on to read two chapters or watch two more programs. And I never did anything like clip my sister's hair or bite her arm. And I never fought with my mother. I always gave in, trusting her judgment more than my own.

This is the main illusion of my adult years: that I was different from my own children.

Oh, for a child who is just like me.

Who is like me? Let him stand up and speak,
/make it evident, and confront me with it.
Is 44:7

Thief in the Night

My children don't want to visit Grandpa anymore. It upsets them when he doesn't remember them or stares off into space and drools. They remember the grandpa that took them fishing and bought them their first bike—who always had time for and was interested in what they had to say. This grandpa is a complete stranger to them. They don't believe he's the same man. Sometimes I think they are right.

I stare in his face and look for the man I remember. He isn't there. I hold his hand and look for some sign of recognition, desperate for some assurance of his love for us. I get none. Instead I try to assure him of our love and care.

Someone came and stole Grandpa away, like a thief in the night. His name was Alzheimer.

Do not cast me aside in my old age; /as my strength fails, do not forsake me. /God, do not stand far from me; /my God, hasten to help me. Ps 71:9, 12

Let Me Help

Beware the words above when spoken by a three-year-old! When my children say those words, what they want to help with are usually things that are beyond their ability for their age. Their "help" ends up meaning more work for me.

So it is with us and God.

So often we mothers want to do the "big" seemingly more "glamorous" things that may be beyond our means rather than the "little" things God sets before us each day. What others are doing always seems more important, more special, than what we are doing.

There is no work more important than what God has already given us.

For if we live, we live for the Lord, and if we die, we die for the Lord; so then, whether we live or die, we are the Lord's. Rom 14:8

To Trust or Not to Trust

My daughter came home from school in tears. It seems her best friends have decided to exclude her. Secrets they had once shared together are now sources of laughter for the "in-group" from which she is "out." Friends she had trusted have proven to be untrustworthy. What's worse is that tomorrow—if they decide to let her back "in"—she will probably entrust herself to those fickle friends again.

Learning to trust is one of the most basic tasks of development. Yet learning *not* to trust is as important.

It may cost us some money or time to find out who is trustworthy, but that's a small price to pay to know the character of our "friends." Jesus paid the price with his life.

What price will my daughter have to pay?

_____

Behold, I am sending you like sheep in the midst of wolves; so be shrewd as serpents and simple as doves. Mt 10:16

Home, Safe Home

Children need a base from which to explore, to go out into an unsafe world. Two-year-olds instinctively know this. They tentatively explore the exciting new world, but then retreat when the world becomes too big and overwhelming.

We all need a secure place where we can go to be ourselves. Where we are loved unconditionally. Where we are rocked and comforted. Where it's OK to cry and be vulnerable. And where it's OK to leave when you are ready to leave.

We all need a mother's lap now and then.

"How many times I yearned to gather your children together as a hen gathers her brood under her wings." Lk 13:34

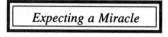

Expecting a Miracle

As a child, I believed that if I only prayed hard enough and waited long enough I would get what I wanted I now realize that God can't be manipulated. I no longer pray for miracles because that's just another way for me to try to manipulate God. It presupposes a God like a mother with a jar full of goodies that can only be coerced out of her rather than like a mother waiting to freely rain blessings on her children.

My attempts to "pray" God into giving me what I want sometimes blinds me to the miracles already occurring in the world: the healings that occur each day with the help of medicine, the wonder of birth, the triumph of people breaking through denial to seek out the help they need, the relief of reconciliation.

So, I no longer pray for miracles. I'm too busy thanking God for the many miracles I see every day.

Moses summoned all Israel and said to them,
'You have seen all that the LORD did in the land
of Egypt before your very eyes to Pharaoh and
all his servants and to all his land; the great
testings your own eyes have seen, and those
great signs and wonders. But not even at the
present day has the LORD yet given you a mind
to understand, or eyes to see, or ears to hear.
Dt 29:1-3

Nettles

Prince Charming had to fight his way through giant nettles and high walls in order to wake Sleeping Beauty. Some children have walls just as high as Sleeping Beauty's, with giant nettles all around them. The walls guard against anyone getting close. The nettles prick anyone who dares to approach them on more than a superficial level. And, if anyone should find a way through the cracks in the walls, the children lash out, pull the drawbridge back up, and slam it shut.

Inside the walls is a scared and lonely child longing for someone to care for her. The wicked witch has created a barrier between her and the world, and now not only can't she break out, she doesn't want to.

Sleeping Beauty doesn't need Prince Charming. She needs a mom.

———————————————

For I am the LORD, your God, who grasp your right hand; /it is I who say to you, "Fear not, I will help you" Is 41:13

One Small Voice

Just when I feel I'm making some headway, something happens. I find enough to get ahead of the bills, then one of the kids comes home sick or with a broken bone and I'm back in the hole. Struggling to make ends meet, I want to give up. The voice of despair howls loudly in my ears, drowning out all other voices.

But one small voice breaks through, quietly, persistently.

"Mom, I'm home. What's for snack?"

My child's voice overcomes the deafening roar of despair and I remember there is more to being a mom than chores. I go on for my children's sake, and my own.

Then the Lord said, "Go outside and stand on the mountain before the Lord; the Lord will be passing by." A strong and heavy wind was rending the mountains and crushing rocks before the Lord—but the Lord was not in the wind. After the wind there was an earthquake— but the Lord was not in the earthquake. After the earthquake there was fire—but the Lord was not in the fire. After the fire there was a tiny whispering sound. When he heard this, Elijah hid his face in his cloak and went and stood at the entrance of the cave. 1 Kgs 19:11-13

Groundhog Day

How I wish I were a groundhog hiding beneath the earth, burrowed under a mantle of snow, popping my head out only to duck back in. I burrow down deeper into my covers only to hear the alarm ring once again. I reach to turn it off and turn back to sleep, but my husband pulls the covers off.

"Rise and shine, sleepyhead," he says.

I groan and pull the covers back. A small face appears at the foot of my bed, and the baby begins to cry. Time to get up.

I hustle my daughter to school then settle with a cup of coffee as I nurse the baby and my toddler watches Sesame Street. I look out the window at the mounds of snow.

How I wish I were a groundhog.

It is the hour now for you to awake from sleep. For our salvation is nearer now than when we first believed; the night is advanced, the day is at hand. Rom 13:11-12

Legacy

What legacy are we mothers leaving our children? Will the world that we leave behind be a safer one for them? Will it be a better place for their children to play? Will our generation be the one to finally end war, hatred, prejudice, pollution? Or will we leave behind a world on the edge of destruction?

We won't single-handedly put an end to thousands of years of hatred. Single-handedly, we won't change human nature, its desire to control, its jealousies and its drive to power. But with God's help, we may change ourselves. We may rise above our selfish natures to true self-giving love, and in doing so we will make a better world for our children and our children's children.

With God's help, we mothers can make a difference.

"Who then can be saved?" Jesus looked at them and said, "For human beings this is impossible, but for God all things are possible." Mt 19:25-26

Decisions, Decisions

My daughter has a terrible time making even the simplest decision. She can spend hours in the library choosing a book or in the grocery store picking out candy.

The only person I know who takes longer to make a decision is me. I have to weigh all sides, look at them over and over again, until finally I throw caution to the wind and plunge right in, disregarding all of my earlier thought processes and going with what "feels" right.

The older I get and the more decisions I have made, the more able I am to see the ramifications of my decisions—which makes it even harder to choose the next time around. I see how the choices I made in my twenties affected me in my thirties. The choice to marry the man I did has made me a different person from the one I would have been with another marriage partner. Our choices about where to live affect not only us, but our children as well.

So, my daughter, make up your mind and get on with it. As quickly as you make one decision, you'll be faced with another.

Do not conform yourself to this age but be
transformed by the renewal of your mind, that
you may discern what is the will of God, what is
good and pleasing and perfect. Rom 12:2

Another Chance

Sometimes I can see my children with the eyes of their grandmother. She doesn't have to raise them, get up with them each night, put up with their sassy mouths. That is for their mother to deal with.

Grandma can't spoil them. They are already perfect to her, and perfection can't be spoiled.

Time can never give back all the things it has taken from her. Still, being a grandmother gives her a chance to love, without all the work and heartache.

You changed my mourning into dancing; /you took off my sackcloth and clothed me with gladness. Ps 30:12

Setting Limits

Life with children is a continuous series of limit setting and limit testing. Children need limits to test. Once those limits are accepted, they rest secure.

One difficult thing about mothering is that limits have to be continuously changed to meet the growing needs of different children, and each time they change they are tested once again.

Have no fear when setting limits, Mom. Don't be disturbed by the constant testing. It is a normal and healthy part of parenting. Your kids will thank you for it—much later!

If I fly with the wings of dawn /and alight beyond the sea, /Even there your hand will guide me, /your right hand hold me fast. Ps 139:9-10

Slamming Doors

I don't believe that God goes around shutting doors in our faces. That would be a cruel God who plays games with us. What's behind door #1, door #2, door #3? We guess, and if we don't guess right we get life slammed in our faces.

I believe it is people who shut doors. They don't want to let God in, because it might mean they'll have to change.

God is busy opening windows, straining to find ways to get in. God never slams the door.

"So now I tell you, have nothing to do with these men, and let them go. For if this endeavor or this activity is of human origin, it will destroy itself. But if it comes from God, you will not be able to destroy them; you may even find yourselves fighting against God."
Acts 5:38-39

Faster than a speeding tricycle,

More powerful than a stuck coat zipper,

Able to leap tall mounds of laundry with a single bound,

It's . . . Supermom!

Supermom's incredible hearing helps her block out all sounds save the near-death knell of her children. Her x-ray vision allows her to look past piles of dirty dishes and dust-balls in the corners. With super fast speed and agility, she maneuvers past toys and clothing throughout the house without a single fall. Equipped with a cup of coffee, her radio turned to her favorite station, she retreats to the tub, settles into the hot water and bubbles, and becomes . . . invisible.

"Come to me, all you who labor and are burdened, and I will give you rest." Mt 11:28

PMS

tense, tension, jittery, jagged nerves

ready to explode

bounce, bounce, bouncing off the wall

like a ball in a pinball machine

run, run, running in circles

like a gerbil in a cage

on a wheel round and round

need to rest but can't

need to sleep but toss and turn

stomach gurgles

breasts swell

brain races

---

*There was a woman afflicted with hemorrhages
for twelve years. She had suffered greatly at
the hands of many doctors and had spent all
that she had. Yet she was not helped but only
grew worse. She had heard about Jesus and
came up behind him in the crowd and touched
his cloak. She said, "If I but touch his clothes,
I shall be cured." Mk 5:25-28*

Roller-Coaster Ride

Some days life seems so melodramatic. Battles of light and darkness, peace versus despair. Pride over one teen's accomplishments disappears when a call comes saying another child is waiting at the police station, picked up for drinking.

This, too, will pass. These years of extremes. This roller-coaster ride. There's peace and serenity beyond the turbulence, if you can just make it through.

Whoever said that being a mother was one boring succession of the same, never had kids.

Every valley shall be filled in, /every mountain and hill shall be made low. /The rugged land shall be made a plain, /the rough country, a broad valley. /Then the glory of the LORD shall be revealed. Is 40:4-5

Dancing in Darkness

I'm in awe of people who always seem to know what they are about at any given time. Who have no doubt what God is calling them to do. Watching a film about Mother Teresa, I was struck by how when she heard God ask her to go to care for the poor of India, she just did it. No mention of months or years of questioning whether this was what God truly wanted.

There are very few mothers like Teresa in this world. Most of us are stuck in the quagmire of our own thought processes: Is this the right thing to do? What about my children? How will this affect them? I know this maternal quagmire all too well. I've spent so much time in it, groping around, trying to see ahead, examining my motivation for doing something lest I do something for myself—or others—that somehow might harm my children.

But there's an alternative to wallowing in this quagmire. It's called dancing in darkness. In the one you are stewing in your own juices, in the other you take the risk. Both ways are difficult, both uncertain, but one leads to despair, the other to hope.

Immediately a dark mist fell upon him, and he went about seeking people to lead him by the hand. Acts 13:11

In Silence

There are hurts buried deep. I hide from them. I hide behind my children, the constant noise and commotion of young life. I hide behind newspapers and magazines, a plenitude of reading material to fill my restless mind. I hide behind the radio and TV, noise to fill my every waking moment.

There are hurts buried deep. Only in silence do they come to the surface. Only in silence do I feel my anguish and cry out, alone, seeking my lost love, my God.

The rest is but a dull ache.

Out of the depths I call to you, LORD; /LORD hear my cry! /May your ears be attentive /to my cry for mercy. Ps 130:1-2

Little Kids, Little Problems, Big Kids . . .

Why is it? They misbehave, they are punished. But we mothers are the ones who pay—whether for the little squabbles of our young children or the more serious offenses of our teens and adult children. The dynamics haven't changed, just the magnitude.

Little kids, little problems; big kids, big problems. It hurts to see our children choose the wrong way. Even if we know they are in the wrong, that they deserve to be punished, we pay. It hurts to see our children hurt.

They ignored my counsel, /they spurned all my reproof; /and in their arrogance they preferred arrogance /and like fools they hated knowledge: /"Now they must eat the fruit of their own way, /and with their own devices be glutted."
Prv 1:30-31

Over Some Dishwater

Where is the one who will take me away from this? From dishpan hands and endless loads of laundry and the constant pick, pick, pick of fighting children? Who will sweep me up and fly me to some island far away from responsibility?

When my children were babies it was an awe-filled experience. It's hard to recapture that now that baby talk has turned into back talk and the echoes of "mo-0-m!" has become a four letter word that resounds in my ears non-stop each day. Now more than ever I need an escape, a romantic interlude with the one I love . . . or even with a stranger! Just to be away and know I exist apart from these children and their constant demands.

Sticky hands reach up to grab my arms, and I divert my attention from the dishwater to the child whose face still bears remnants of chocolate valentine candy. She hands me a homemade valentine with glue still wet. I try not to notice the mess she made on the kitchen table as I wipe my hands, hug her and hang up the valentine in one of the few bare spots left on my refrigerator door.

"Thank you, sweetie," I tell her as she scoots off to play.

Arise, my beloved, my beautiful one, and come!
Song 2:13

The Snap Demons

Some days I wake up in a bad mood for no apparent reason. The problems of the previous day have spilled over into my night even as I slept, wearing me out, bringing out feelings that lay repressed. I wake up a grouch and snap at the kids, snap at my husband, snap at myself, until I'm finally able to find the time to snap out of it.

I wonder, too, what cares lurk in my children's young minds, waiting to disturb their sleep? They also wake up grouchy, snapping at each other, and at me, again for no apparent reason.

Perhaps they too are visited by snap demons in their dreams.

Then Pharaoh woke up, to find it was only a dream. Next morning his spirit was agitated. So he summoned all the magicians and sages of Egypt and recounted his dreams to them; but no one could interpret his dreams for him. Gn 41:7-8

Recycling Problems

Other people recycle newspapers. I recycle problems. The same problems over and over again. They keep recurring in my life. Only the names and faces change. I try so hard to break the pattern, only to find that the moment I think I've made it I've stumbled into another trap of my own making.

I believe in a God who heals, who helps us break out of all that is unhealthy and that keeps us slaves to sin. This belief comes in conflict with my experience of recycling problems. I want to believe I'm healed, growing, making important changes in my life. And then I fall flat on my face again.

Still, I believe God heals me.

Putting spittle on his eyes he laid his hands on him and asked, "Do you see anything?" Looking up he replied, "I see people looking like trees and walking." Then he laid hands on his eyes a second time and he saw clearly; his sight was restored and he could see everything distinctly. Mk 8:23-25

Maternal Waiting

There's something wrong. I can see it on my son's face. I can sense it. I haven't been his mother for so many years without knowing a few things about him. What are the new struggles he is grappling with? I long to ask him. I want so badly to know, to talk to him, to reassure him of my love, to help him . . . but I can't. I have to wait for him to come to me.

What a painful game maternal waiting is. Far more difficult than nine months of pregnancy. That was just the preparation for what was to come. To sit back and wait when I suspect something is wrong, to honor his growing manhood—what a difficult thing to do.

Just so God waits for us. Waits for us to come with all our problems, all our concerns.

How long will we keep God waiting?

I wait with longing for the LORD, /my soul waits for his word. /My soul looks for the LORD more than sentinels for daybreak. Ps 130:5-6

The Tooth Fairy

"Mommy, I really want to know. Is there really a tooth fairy?"

"What do you think?"

"Well, I believe in the tooth fairy, but I want to know if it's true. Is there a tooth fairy, or do you and Daddy leave the money?"

I can put him off no longer. He wants to know. He's ready to know.

"No, there isn't really a tooth fairy."

"Waaa," he sobs into his pillow.

He answered, "I heard you in the garden; but I was afraid, because I was naked, so I hid myself." Then he asked, "Who told you that you were naked? You have eaten, then, from the tree of which I had forbidden you to eat!" Gn 3:10-11

The Squeaky Wheel

I've often wondered about the good shepherd leaving the ninety-nine to find the one lost sheep. I've wondered what the ninety-nine who were abandoned thought!

What of the mother who leaves her children to seek out the lost child, or who allows the one child who is acting out and in trouble to take up all her time and energy?

"The squeaky wheel gets the grease," my mother used to say.

How unfair to the other wheels.

But there will be glory, honor, and peace for everyone who does good, Jew first and then Greek. There is no partiality with God. Rom 2:10-11

View from the Top

Somehow it was supposed to be more fun than this. It wasn't supposed to cost so much. She was the "new woman." She could have it all. But she didn't get it.

She's made it to the top, but the view isn't so great.

I took the small scroll from the angel's hand and swallowed it. In my mouth it was like sweet honey, but when I had eaten it, my stomach turned sour. Rev 10:10

> *Changes*

It's not so much that I'm opposed to change as that I'm just plain tired! I'd be all for change if it didn't require any work on my part.

Even positive changes require work. Buying a new car means getting used to a whole new way of driving. Where are the windshield wipers and the lights, and how do I get this radio to tune in the stations I want to hear? It means learning a whole new set of quirks when I was used to the ones in the old car. Is this shiny new car with the clean upholstery and carpet really worth trading in old Boomer with the dents, nicks, rust spots, stains on the upholstery and blackened, sticky carpet? Besides, when the inevitable happens and the kids tramp across the seat with muddy shoes, I will feel a responsibility to yell at them.

I'm for change, as long as I'm not the one who has to change.

Behold, I tell you a mystery. We shall not all fall asleep, but we will all be changed, in an instant, in the blink of an eye, at the last trumpet. For the trumpet will sound, the dead will be raised incorruptible, and we shall be changed. 1 Cor 15:51-52

The Cycle

The phone rings. It's her again.

"Yes, come on over," I tell her, hang up and sigh. She's coming over with her two sons. I get out of bed. I know her cycle too well. The pressure has built up till there has been an explosion. Later, her husband will apologize, will be contrite, will buy flowers . . . and she will forgive him. She will tell herself that this time things will be different.

I wonder about her sons, what they must feel when they see their father that way, when they hear their mother's yelling and see her bruises. I ask her: What are you teaching your sons? That it's all right to hit their future wives?

My oldest daughter comes downstairs to see what's going on. I send her back to bed, reassuring her that it's nothing. She knows I'm lying. She knows what is going on. I wonder, what am I teaching her?

"Saul, Saul, why are you persecuting me?"
Acts 9:4

Depression

Anger turned inward, that's what they say. Why are women so prone to depression? Men turn their anger outward, at objects, people, places, circumstances beyond themselves. Women turn their anger inward, where it festers until it's no longer recognizable. It's been so long since I've felt real, good, solid, clean anger. I wouldn't even recognize it anymore.

Women are taught to suppress our anger, yet it still retains its destructive powers. All of it is unleashed upon ourselves.

Depression: lives wasted, lives unlived.

Be angry but do not sin; do not let the sun set on your anger, and do not leave room for the devil. Eph 4:26.

Yearning

My soul yearns for one I do not know. In quiet I await my love and he comes to me. In the mighty wind, in the majestic storm, in lightning and thunder, in the gentle breeze, he comes to me and calls me his own, his beloved, his child.

My soul yearns for his embrace, for his touch. But a touch of his breath and I am lost, overwhelmed, in awe.

I long to call his name, but he remains nameless. I long to feel his caress, know his love, see him face to face.

My being thirsts for God, the living God.
/When can I go and see the face of God?
Ps 42:3

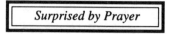

Surprised by Prayer

I've never been one for rising early for prayer (I'd much rather meditate on the mystery of sleep), but since the birth of my children I've been up at all hours of the night, rocking crying babies, chasing away nightmares, bringing drinks of water, and escorting three-year-olds to the bathroom. As I lie awake, struggling to get back to sleep, these hours become prayer time.

At times, my life is totally disrupted by the simple words, "Mommy, I don't feel good." Suddenly, plans have to be set aside, schedules juggled, and busyness forcibly brought to a halt. In the midst of what was to be a busy week, I find unplanned-for, unexpected, quiet time to pray.

Children force mothers to pray, and they often provide the opportunity. The spirituality of a mother is not one that can be too structured. God breaks into our lives, catches us on the run, and demands time with us. Sometimes it is when we least expect it, and when we are least prepared for it.

Lord, my heart is not proud; /nor are my eyes haughty. /I do not busy myself with great matters, /with things too sublime for me. /Rather, I have stilled my soul, /hushed it like a weaned child. /Like a weaned child on its mother's lap, /so is my soul within me. Ps 131:1-2

> *Energized*

Particles moving in an absolute vacuum will keep on and on and on at the same rate of speed without stop. My children don't live in a vacuum, but some days it seems as though they do. They never stop. Their batteries never run down. They dance circles around me as I lie in a heap on the floor.

"Go away," I say. "Mommy needs her nap even if you don't."

Children. If only we could harness their energy, we could fuel the world.

Have I the strength of stones, /or is my flesh of bronze? Jb 6:12

Tantrums

I was prepared for the terrible twos, forewarned and therefore forearmed. What I wasn't prepared for were the ferocious fours . . . or the feisty fives. Somehow I thought if I survived the terrible twos I'd have it made—at least until the terrifying teens. But no, the tantrums just get more vocal.

Thank God, they do go underground for a while during the relative calm of the grade school years, only to re-emerge in full force at the onset of puberty.

Children. They keep going. On and on and on . . .

Have I no helper, and has advice deserted me?
Jb 6:13

And On and On

To think there was a time when my children couldn't speak at all. Doesn't seem possible now. Now it's always one more song to sing, one more story to tell, one more accomplishment to show off. It never ends, especially at bedtime. They just go on and on and on.

"Mommy, can I tell you just one more thing?"

"No, let me tell you something, young lady."

"But, Mom!"

Like the winter, like this dreary month of February, they just keep going. On and on and on . . .

I have been assigned months of misery, /and troubled nights have been told off for me.
Jb 7:3

And On

"Mom, will you write down my story for me?"

"As long as it's not too long. I don't have a lot of time."

"This is about a boy in a boat. A storm starts and tips the boat over. The boy and his boat land on an island. There is a king on the island. The boy asks him to fix his boat. The king says he will, but first the boy has to give him something. The boy asks what. The king says he must rescue the princess from the wicked witch and bring her back. So the boy and his dog rescue the princess, and the king fixes his boat. Then they all go fishing in the boat and catch a magic fish . . . "

"Honey, when is this story going to end?"

"Oh, it won't be long, Mommy. The magic fish grants him three wishes . . . "

On and on and on . . .

_____

How long will you utter such things? /The words from your mouth are like a mighty wind! Jb 8:2

Dear God

I appreciate the fact that my kids came complete with self-recharging batteries. I also appreciate the fact that no assembly was required.

But what I don't understand is why you would give such a precious and complex gift without including an instruction manual. I can figure out most of the things myself. What I can't handle are the daily squabbles over food, clothing, bedtime, and everything in-between.

Perhaps if all I had to do was work with them eight to ten hours each day (with lunch break, of course), then I wouldn't need instructions. But these kids are a twenty-four hour job. And just when I think I've got the operation down pat, the rules change and I'm left scrambling once again to find those operating instructions I know you must have sent with all their other important papers, such as their life insurance policies and lifetime guarantees.

Which brings up another subject, Dear God. Where are those guarantees?

The aim of this instruction is love from a pure heart, a good conscience, and a sincere faith.
1 Tm 1:5

| *Survival* |

I used to think of mothering as a lifetime of gently and lovingly building young minds, of baking cookies and kissing booboos and having meaningful conversations on important issues.

I now realize that a large part of mothering is simple survival. I put on my combat gear each day and collapse each night in peace with the knowledge that my family has survived another day.

I live each day, one day at a time, thankful to have survived. Sometimes, only sometimes, those gentle images of my earlier years break through into reality. They are all the sweeter for having been earned at such a high price.

———————————————

And whoever does not provide for relatives and especially family members has denied the faith and is worse than an unbeliever. 1 Tm 5:8

Special Child

Who is this less-than-perfect baby? It couldn't be hers. There must have been some mistake. What did she do to deserve him? How does she care for him? He's so different. He'll never be like the other kids. He'll need special schools, special care.

Her son cries, and she picks him up. His crying ceases as his mother cradles him in her arms.

Some things are not different.

"See that you do not despise one of these little ones, for I say to you that their angels in heaven always look upon the face of my heavenly Father." Mt 18:10

$$\boxed{\textit{AIDS}}$$

A transfusion? Sure, if we have to. But what is this paper I have to sign? My daughter is not even a day old. She's far too young for me to have to be concerned about some sexually transmitted disease. And yet I have to sign a paper stating I recognize that the risk of AIDS comes with all blood transfusions. So I sign it.

Why do I have to be confronted by this scourge? Why should a simple transfusion—which means the difference between life or death for my daughter—also bring the threat of death to her in her innocence?

Still, I sign the paper. The risk is small. We have to accept it. But why now? Why so soon? Why couldn't I put off facing this reality? Why couldn't I continue to deny that AIDS already affects me personally.

Give me back my denial!

And I too, when born, inhaled the common air, /and fell upon the kindred earth; /wailing, I uttered that first sound common to all. /In swaddling clothes and with constant care I was nurtured. /For no king has any different origin or birth, /but one is the entry into life for all; /and in one same way they all leave it.
Wis 7:3-6

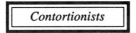

Contortionists

His little rear end sticks up like a mound, raising the covers in his crib. I don't know why he sleeps that way. Chest on the mattress, mouth open, butt in the air. It strikes me as so uncomfortable, but every effort I make to put him in what to me would be a more comfortable position is in vain.

Children are such contortionists! They strike me as being so flexible that their bones are more like jelly than rock. They dance and run and bend in ways unbelievable to my hardening body.

But children are flexible only in appearance. They can bend and shape, but only so far.

And we can break them if we bend them too far.

_____

By patience is a ruler persuaded, /and a soft tongue will break a bone. Prv 25:15

Correspondence

It's been so long since I've caught up on my correspondence. Even the concept of "caught up" seems ridiculous. Friends must think I've forgotten them, but I haven't forgotten. They remain precious parts of my memory.

Mothers lose touch with so many friends. The burden of keeping up with them is too much.

So many letters unwritten—lost amidst bills, family records, school papers. Lost amidst the responsibilities of family.

Will my friends ever forgive me?

Your own friend and your father's friend forsake not ; / . . . better is a neighbor near at hand than a brother far away. Prv 27:10

The Perfect Mother

There she is again. That perfect mother with her perfect child. She's so calm and composed as she walks through the grocery store. Every time the child asks for something, the mother calmly says yes or no and the child accepts her explanation.

I hate her.

I snarl for no reason at all at my son, lest he even think to ask for anything.

Meanwhile the perfect mother loads her cart with diapers, letting me know there are more at home, probably equally obedient.

If only I could entice her child to knock over a cereal display!

———————————

Set a guard, Lord, before my mouth, /a gatekeeper at my lips. /Do not let my heart incline to evil /or yield to any sin. /I will never feast upon /the fine food of evildoers.
Ps 141:3-4

Motherhood Denied

Everywhere she looks are mothers. Pregnant mothers, mothers pushing strollers, mothers herding two or three small children, mothers with teenage children, mothers of adults. She doesn't want to hear their complaints of backaches or sleepless nights or quarreling children. If they only knew how readily she could change places with them.

Everywhere she looks are reminders of her own defective body, unable to bring another life into this world.

She'll find other ways to nurture life, everyone assures her. She can always adopt, others say.

But how she longs to feel that quickening life within her, to experience that ultimate womanly experience—childbirth—denied to her forever.

In her bitterness she prayed to the LORD, weeping copiously, and she made a vow, promising: "O LORD of hosts, if you look with pity on the misery of your handmaid, if you remember me and do not forget me, if you give your handmaid a male child, I will give him to the LORD for as long as he lives." 1 Sm 1:10-11

Paul—the Jewish Mother

Paul must have been a mother. I know this is a physical impossibility, yet he watched over the communities that he founded like a mother hen or wolf. His words echo those of many a good mother.

"You know how I spent the whole time I was with you . . . ."

"You know that I didn't hold back anything that would be of help to you . . . ."

"To Jews and Gentiles alike I gave solemn warnings that they should turn from their sins . . . ."

"I only know that in every city the Holy Spirit has warned me that prison and troubles wait for me . . . and what thanks did I get?"

Thank you, Mother Paul.

Do you not recall that while I was still with you I told you these things? 2 Thes 2:5

Dandelions of Spring

Her child is gone. Dead for almost six months. She was too young. Just a teenager. Her empty room a constant reminder.

It seems that only yesterday she was running to her mother on tiny toddler legs with the first dandelions of spring.

Oh, to fight with her daughter one more time over clothes, boys, dates, homework. How precious even those arguments are now. To have her back for just a day. To say "I love you" one more time.

The king was shaken, and went up to the room over the city gate to weep. He said as he wept, '"My son Absalom! My son, my son Absalom! If only I had died instead of you, Absalom, my son, my son!" 2 Sm 19:1

Pedestal

Don't put me on a pedestal children . . . the fall is too great and painful. Don't idolize me or place me next to God. I don't want or deserve such stature. Just let me be me and loved for who I am.

The role of mother is so filled with expectations. One minute she is the all-powerful goddess who fulfills all her children's dreams, the next she is a wicked witch who denies them everything. Children can't see the human behind the role. It's beyond their capacity.

If only my children could accept me as I truly am.

The apostles Barnabas and Paul tore their garments when they heard this and rushed out into the crowd, shouting, "Men, why are you doing this? We are of the same nature as you, human beings." Acts 14:14-15

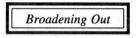

Broadening Out

    The task of early motherhood is one of narrowing in, of making choices that define one's self. How many children will we have? How will we parent? Should we stay home with them or work outside the home?

    The task of mature motherhood is to broaden out. Within those choices we have made, we must expand our horizons. Shall we start a new career? Go back to school? Write that book we have always put off?

    This broadening out process is a painful one, and yet necessary if we are to mother with a sense of integrity.

Neither in my youth, nor in old age, /have I ever seen the just abandoned /or their children begging bread. /The just always lend generously, /and their children become a blessing. Ps 37:25-26

Mind Reading

I'm a mind reader *par excellence*. It wasn't something I trained for or inherited. It came automatically with the birth of my first child and grew with each subsequent birth.

As tempting as it might be to amaze all with my powers of mental perception, however, I don't play this game. Even though I know what the problem is, I make my children verbalize it to me. You see, mothers who make it easy on their children by reading their minds for them set them up for a lifetime of inability to express their needs. We do them an injustice.

The world is full of adults who don't know how to ask for what they want or need. The world is full of adults who don't know how to communicate basic desires. They all had mothers who read their minds.

"I tell you, ask and you will receive; seek and you will find; knock and the door will be opened to you." Lk 11:9

Roadblocks

Everywhere I turn I see roadblocks—supposed dead ends telling me to give up.

No one is making it easy for me. Juggling schedules, finding babysitters, trying to study, and all for what? Will there even be a place for me when I'm through? Will they be open to a woman, an older one, in this line of work? What other obstacles will there be then?

Roadblocks can be reasons to give up, to give in and settle for less. Or they can force us to be creative, to take leaps of faith over the top. They can be the friction against which graphite is turned into diamond.

Everywhere I turn I see roadblocks, challenges taking me on detours, down roads I never thought I'd travel. I'm learning to enjoy them.

We know that all things work for good for those who love God, who are called according to his purpose. Rom 8:28

Hidden Loss

She can never regain her lost childhood. Never retrieve what was taken from her. Not just the loss of innocence, but the loss of self. The crushing blow to a fragile, developing ego.

A victim of childhood sexual abuse. In silence she suffers her hidden loss.

It happened to her. But never to her children.

———————————————

None shall hurt or destroy on all my holy mountain, says the LORD. Is 65:25

> *No!*

I shoo them away, angry with their incessant demands.

How often are our prayers like this, unreasonable requests to a parent God? Are we any more graceful about accepting God's "no" than our children are about accepting ours?

Can we ever learn to just *be* with God?

———————————————

"If God so clothes the grass in the field that grows today and is thrown into the oven tomorrow, will he not much more provide for you, O you of little faith?" Lk 12:28

Unwanted Children

Another baby found in a trash bin, the paper reports. Oh, God, what I wouldn't give for that little baby, that precious life. I'd adopt her right along with my own children. We'd have to squeeze, but we'd find room

I'll take all the unwanted babies. Put them in my arms.

If only their mothers knew. There are no unwanted children. Only children who haven't yet found their homes.

In Ramah is heard the sound of moaning, /of bitter weeping! /Rachel mourns her children, /she refuses to be consoled /because her children are no more. Jer 31:15

A Care-Less Society

"Who cares?" is the current catch phrase for my children. They lose a shoe, "Who cares?" They rip a magazine or book, "Who cares?"

"I care," I tell them. How do I teach them to care for the good things that they have?

We live in a care-less society. We toss our clothes, our toys, our furniture, when they get a little dirty or soiled. We don't even care to protect them because we can always buy new ones. And our society encourages us to buy more. Why spend time and energy trying to repair something that's damaged or broken?

But we've only one planet. We can't buy another when this one has been destroyed.

Thus should one regard us: as servants of Christ and stewards of the mysteries of God. Now it is of course required of stewards that they be found trustworthy. 1 Cor 4:1-2

The Porch Swing, Part 1

Each day, my husband walks around the lake near our town, looking at the signs of thaw. It's that awkward time of year—not cold enough for ice fishing, not warm enough to take out a boat. He plays with his fishing gear in the basement, cleaning it, trying it out in anticipation of spring.

My daughter awaits her graduation. She's ready to be done with school, anxious to go on to new ventures, but she's not free just yet. She waits in limbo, between the ending of one phase of her life and the beginning of another.

My son's voice squeaks high then low. He gazes in the mirror looking for any sign of peach fuzz that will tell him he's becoming a man.

My sister-in-law waddles to her job each day, awaiting her due date this spring.

I dust off my porch swing from where it sits stored in the basement, carry it to the back porch, and sit awhile.

"Look down, then, from heaven, your holy abode, and bless your people Israel and the soil you have given us in the land flowing with milk and honey." Dt 26:15

Perfection

Why are women so obsessed with appearances? So unhappy with the bodies God gave us? Ready to go to any length to change what we were born with?

We powder and paint ourselves, shave our legs and pits, exercise and diet, all in search of that elusive perfect shape—the long-legged model look that most of us can never achieve because we aren't made that way. And when that doesn't work we have plastic surgery—decrease the size of our noses, increase the size of our breasts, a tuck here and a nip there.

God made us all so wonderfully different, with plump bodies made for bearing babies and nurturing, with stretch marks and bulges here and there, fat thighs, knobby knees, crooked noses, thin lips, small or bulbous breasts, fat hips, flat chests. God made us and God made us wondrously. Why do we feel compelled to improve on perfection?

Why are you anxious about clothes? Learn from the way the wild flowers grow. They do not work or spin. But I tell you that not even Solomon in all his splendor was clothed like one of them. Mt 6:28-29

I Have to Go

I gulp when I see the dinky plane pulling up to my gate. Not a 747 or a DC10, but a tiny commuter seating a dozen people at most. This is not what I had bargained for when I agreed to become a mother!

Still my child needs me, so I'm going. I bought a full-priced ticket on the first flight out. I will do whatever is necessary to be at my child's side.

I swallow deep, make sure I have a supply of gum in my purse, and climb aboard. I bury my head in a book and try to pretend I don't feel anything as the plane takes off. I try to quiet my churning stomach.

My child needs me. I have to go.

But the Lord answered me, /Say not, "I am too young." /To whomever I send you, you shall go; /whatever I command you, you shall speak. /Have no fear before them, /because I am with you to deliver you, says the Lord. Jer 1:7-8

Tears, Part 1

Some days I just feel sad for no apparent reason. I cry tears not because of any hurt or sorrowful incident. They are tears that come and go spontaneously.

It's kind of comforting to think that maybe my sadness has nothing to do with my own selfish whims. Perhaps my tears are caused by a greater awareness of the pain in the world—that somehow I am tapping into God's own grief.

Not every ache needs to be analyzed.

Some things just are.

Speak to them this word: /"Let my eyes stream with tears /day and night, without rest, /Over the great destruction which overwhelms /the virgin daughter of my people, /over her incurable wound." Jer 14:17

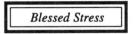

Blessed Stress

How do you deal with the tension of being a mom? The experts recommend vigorous physical exercise. Go for a walk, ride a bike, pound a pillow . . .

The most stressful part of my day is getting the kids off to school each morning.

So afterwards I stay home and ride my exercise bike.

I've lost ten pounds since I started doing this.

Oh, blessed stress!

I will not give vent to my blazing anger, /I will not destroy Ephraim again; /for I am God and not man, /the Holy One present among you; /I will not let the flames consume you. Hos 11:9

Mother/Daughter

There is something special in the mother-daughter bond. There is none closer, and because of that closeness it is fraught with tension. Maybe we're afraid that if we didn't fight we'd forget we are two different people.

Daughters will scratch out the eyes of anyone who suggests we are anything like our mothers—until we finally make lives of our own, have children of our own, and are confident enough in ourselves to admit we are very like our moms.

And then we have daughters and the process repeats itself.

See, everyone who is fond of proverbs will say of you, 'Like mother, like daughter.' Ez 16:44

Nature's Cruel Trick

One more blast. Snow pants that had been put away are brought back out: boots, mittens and hats make an encore performance. Children return inside. Windows are shut again. The TV goes back on.

I have no more ideas for inside entertainment. I've exhausted my winter store. I have no energy to make yet another cup of hot chocolate or organize another sledding expedition. I don't care to build any more snowmen or snow forts.

Nature's cruel trick on mothers—a false spring.

———————————————

Lead me out of my prison, /that I may give thanks to your name. Ps 142:8

Time

If I had all the time in the world, I could wait patiently while my girls go through every article of clothing in their drawers before deciding what they want to wear. I'd be more patient when the person at the check-out ahead of me has several items that require price checks. I wouldn't mind repeating myself one hundred times each day. It wouldn't matter that, every time I'm ready to go out the door, my kids think of ten things that require my urgent attention.

But I don't have all the time in the world.

Unlike God, who knows no boundaries and who is limitless, mothers are limited by time and space. We rush, make mistakes, and have to do over what we just did, taking up more of our precious time. We have a limited amount of time to hug our children, to watch them grow, to guide them in the paths we want them to follow.

_____

Teach us to count our days aright, /that we may gain wisdom of heart. Ps 90:12

The Over-Tired Mother

Now would be a good time for a nanny to show up. Now that I'm exhausted from all this "quality time" with my kids. They are over-tired, but I'm even more over-tired. My children can't seem to comprehend this.

I need my space. Instead of giving me that space my kids continue to hang on me, demanding more attention.

Where is the book on how to deal with over-tired mothers? And how do I get my children to read it?

I say, "If only I had wings like a dove /that I might fly away and find rest. /Far away I would flee; /I would stay in the desert. /I would soon find a shelter /from the raging wind and storm." Ps 55:7-9

Fear

Doesn't mother nature know it's supposed to be spring? What of those poor flowers, popping up despite the late snow, misled by earlier spring-like weather into believing it was time to sprout?

And what of these teenagers of mine, misled by tufts of facial hair or a set of car keys into thinking they are ready for the adult world?

I fear for both.

"This shall be a sign for you: /this year you shall eat the aftergrowth, /next year, what grows of itself; /But in the third year, sow and reap, /plant vineyards and eat their fruit! /The remaining survivors of the house of Judah /shall again strike root below and bear fruit above. /For out of Jerusalem shall come a remnant, /and from Mount Zion, survivors. /The zeal of the LORD of hosts shall do this."
2 Kgs 19:29-31

Spring Break

The phone rings. It's my son in college.

"Mom, I'll be coming home next week."

"What about your camping trip?"

"Got called off. Besides I've got a ton of laundry to get done. You don't mind, do you?"

"No, of course not."

Thank you, God, for spring break.

When Esau looked about, he saw the women and children. "Who are these with you?" he asked. Jacob answered, "They are the children whom God has graciously bestowed on your servant." Gn 33:5

Making Up

"Good night, I love you." With those simple words I try to repair the damage of the day. Damage from fights at school or the peer pressure and criticism that is part of every child's life. From tests not passed or feelings hurt when ostracized on the playground. From their mother's nagging to pick up their clothes, clean their rooms, do their homework, eat their vegetables. With those magic words I try to make up for the times I was too busy to listen or to play.

All mothers need to tell their children they love them every day. Not all of us get the chance.

And a voice came from the heavens, "You are my beloved Son; with you I am well pleased." Mk 1:11

The Right Thing

My teenage son is ringing the doorbell. It's three A.M.

"Hey, Mom, open up. Why is the door locked?"

"I told you our home is locked at midnight. You can go to any one of the addresses on the sheet of paper attached to the door."

"Come on, Mom, cut it out. Open the door."

"The door is locked for the night."

What does a mother do when she's exhausted every measure? When she's tried everything within her power, to no avail? When she's concluded what she is dealing with is beyond her ability to manage? When even prayer fails and all she can do is throw herself into God's arms and hope she's done the right thing?

So humble yourselves under the mighty hand of God, that he may exalt you in due time. Cast all your worries on him because he cares for you. 1 Pt 5:6-7

April 1

The Mother's Corollary

The Mother's Corollary to Murphy's Law is that the minute the phone rings, pandemonium will occur. Whether they are glued in front of the TV, busy coloring pictures, or even asleep, there's something about knowing Mom is talking to another adult that drives children crazy.

They can sense that Mom is somehow less willing or able to watch, listen, or discipline. Now is the time to quietly draw that mural they've always wanted to do on the wall; to get even with their siblings for snitching; to try out the elasticity of the new furniture; to watch the forbidden TV show; to water fight in the bathroom; to flush the action figures down the toilet; to pull hair and scream and run in circles as Mommy calmly tries to finish her conversation.

Then Mommy hangs up the phone. They head for the hills; and Mommy reaches for the aspirin.

Wisdom instructs her children /and admonishes those who seek her. Sir 4:11

Stepmother

Stepmother. What an awful word! Was there ever a story of a kind, caring, loving stepmother?

Yet a stepmother is still a mother. A mother by choice. A mother who knew what the children were like *before* she agreed to mother them.

Maybe it's time to write some new stories.

The woman therefore took the child and nursed it. When the child grew, she brought him to Pharoah's daughter, who adopted him as her son and called him Moses; for she said, "I drew him out of the water." Ex 2:9-10

Trust

"You know, Mommy, in cartoons when someone steps off of a cliff they don't fall until they look down. It's not like that in real life."

No, it isn't, I hasten to assure my five-year-old son lest he decide to try it out for himself. But then I remember Peter walking on the water. He didn't sink until he looked down and realized what he was doing. And I wonder, isn't most mothering like that? It's only when we realize that there is no ground underneath us that we start to fall.

Whether we like it or not, there are a lot of things that mothers have to accept on trust. That doesn't mean it has to be blind trust, but trust we must. The only alternative is to sink like a rock.

Peter said to him in reply "Lord, if it is you, command me to come to you on the water."
Mt 14:28

The Passive-Aggressive Mother

The passive-aggressive mother does not know how to come out and ask for what she wants. She controls through manipulation and innuendo. Children never know where they stand with her because she will never tell them. She says one thing to their faces, another behind their backs. She finds little ways to undermine whatever they hope to accomplish. She has the ability to make her husband into the bad guy.

Some people claim women are more prone to passive-aggressive behavior than men. I don't know about this. I just know that passive-aggressive mothers need help.

"Sincere are all the words of my mouth, /no one of them is wily or crooked." Prv 8:8

Dance of Intimacy

In mature adult relationships, there is an understanding that intimacy is a dance of getting close and pulling apart. The most exciting moments are necessarily followed by separation. No relationship can endure constant togetherness. And so there develops in a marriage a natural flow of coming together and letting go. Couples have no need to cling to any one experience.

Not so with children. Their relationships aren't a dance but a bear hug. Children cling to the good time, never wanting it to end, until the good time becomes a nightmare of screaming over-stimulation. The warm motherly embrace then becomes a refuge, from which they likewise refuse to embark.

How do we teach our children to let go?

Then David, girt with a linen apron, came dancing before the LORD with abandon, as he and all the Israelites were bringing up the ark of the LORD with shouts of joy and to the sound of the horn. 2 Sam 6:14-15

Witch Mom, Part 1

"You don't know how I feel. Nobody knows how I feel."

How early our children learn to manipulate. How does a mother deal with it? I'm psychologized out! I'm so tired of being sensitive to my children's needs and not wanting to disrespect their feelings. My children know this and use it to their advantage. They have my number. They know just what to say to get those old guilt wheels turning.

Enter Witch Mom. If this is what I have to be, then so be it. Sometimes kids don't need pop psychology. Sometimes Mom needs to be more cop than counselor.

"So now, O children, listen to me; /instruction and wisdom do not reject!" Prv 8:32-33

Witch Hunters

When I use the term "Witch Mom," I don't mean to join in the persecution of women who are "different" or "difficult."

Who are the modern day witches? Anyone who dares to be different, who fights against the status quo.

Who are the modern day witch hunters? People, ordinary people, who are afraid. It only takes a few to work on the fears of the masses to instigate another witch hunt. These people look for bogeywomen and scapegoats, for any excuse to blame someone or something outside of themselves for their problems.

I want to teach my children to dare to be different, but what a risk to take. How do I do that without throwing them to the witch hunters?

Many shepherds have ravaged my vineyard, /have trodden my heritage underfoot; /The portion that delighted me they have turned /into a desert waste. Jer 12:10

Mom Making

Hey, Mom. What's happening? I'm just floating around down here in this bag. It's great. What's that gurgling I hear? Dinner?! That means I should get what you just ate in an hour or two. Wonder what's on the menu tonight?

Do you know I'm in here yet? Can you hear me? I can hear you. I already know the sound of your voice, the beat of your heart. I can't wait to see your face. But I like it in here. It's warm and cozy. Maybe I'll stay here forever. Or at least for a while longer.

It's a big responsibility I have—making a mere woman into a mother. I don't know whether I'm up to the job.

"And this will be a sign for you: you will find an infant wrapped in swaddling clothes and lying in a manger." Lk 2:12

Packing Up

The child psychologists say that children should be involved and under foot during a move. After all, their whole little world is being put into boxes, and they have a tremendous fear of losing something important to them. So much for getting rid of all those excess toys that clutter the hall closet by conveniently leaving some behind!

Their eagle eyes watch every small item. Toys they had forgotten they even had become treasures they can't live without. And so I cart box after box of broken toys to my new home. Some day they'll grow up and I'll be free of this clutter, I tell myself. When they leave, out will go their years of accumulation.

Meanwhile, I go through my own possessions with an eye to getting rid of some of it. I look through the boxes packed away in closets and basement. I discover old friends.

"I just might use this someday," I think. "Oh, look, my favorite . . ."

"Do not store up for yourselves treasures on earth, where moth and decay destroy, and thieves break in and steal. But store up treasures in heaven, where neither moth nor decay destroys, nor thieves break in and steal. For where your treasure is, there also will your heart be." Mt 6:19-21

Icing on the Cake

All mothers have a reason for being here, but sometimes I wonder if the reason has nothing to do with what we may think it is but rather may be to accomplish some small, obscure act whose impact we can't recognize at all. Yet we continue beating ourselves over the head, trying to do more and more. Or we get upset any time someone or some event interferes with what we believe God wants us to do with our lives.

As a recovering over-achiever, I find some comfort in the idea that I've already done the one thing God wanted me to do. Anything after that is icing on the cake, right? I don't have to keep trying to achieve more and more. I can be happy with who I am.

And so, before I rush out in pursuit of yet another goal or to start another project, I pray for the grace to stop, look and listen. I'm reminded of yet another saying I teach my children:

> "Stop, look and listen before you cross
> the street.
> Use your eyes, use your ears, and *then*
> use your feet."

"I know indeed how to live in humble circum-stances; I know also how to live with abun-dance. Phil 4:12

Absolutes

"Mommy, how come you never take us to the park?"

"But we always get two pieces of candy before bedtime."

"It's been forever since we had ice cream."

Welcome to the children's world of absolutes. There are no sometimes, or in-betweens, just always and never, and forever.

Two can play at this game, though.

"How come you never brush your teeth?"

"But we always clean our room before we go to bed."

"It's been forever since you washed your hair."

"You never say thank you."

"To what shall I compare this generation? It is like children who sit in marketplaces and call to one another, 'We played the flute for you, but you did not dance, we sang a dirge but you did not mourn.' " Mt 11:16-17

Car Accident

She drove to the hospital in pouring rain. The windshield wipers fought back the tears from the sky. Outside she was calm and composed. Inside fear rampaged through her mind. Dear God, let them be all right. Don't think, just drive, she told herself.

She pulled into the parking lot, rushed to the emergency room. She found them there, bandaged, sore, a little disoriented, but OK.

"Hi, Mom," the boys smiled weakly, sheepishly. One sat up in a wheel chair. The other was lying down. Her husband sat next to them, a bandage on his head.

"We're all right," he reassured her. "They're just gonna do a few more tests before they discharge us."

How fragile is a mother's life.

Like cool water to one faint from thirst /is good news from a far country. Prv 25:25

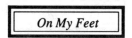

On My Feet

"Hi, Mom," my eight year old son greets me at the end of my work day. "You need some help with the groceries?"

"I sure do," I tell him gratefully.

"You sit down and put your feet up," he says. "I'll put the pizza in the oven."

"You don't have to," I reply weakly. "Go out and play if you want."

"I don't want to. I want to fix supper." I accept his offer guiltily.

Where did I get this mature young man for a son? Am I robbing him of his childhood?

I get back up on my aching feet and join him in the kitchen. "Here, let me do that."

"Let the children come to me, and do not prevent them; for the kingdom of heaven belongs to such as these." Mt 19:14

Agonize

This is only the second time my son forgot his backpack all year. The first time I drove over with it and told him I wouldn't do it again. So now it happened again. I had to be out and about this morning anyway. It wouldn't be that big an inconvenience. But then, what would that teach him? Would my bringing him the backpack today mean trouble down the road? Will I be creating problems for myself if I don't push the issue of responsibility now?

I rush by his school. By this time he has completely forgotten about the backpack and is outside playing with the other kids. He hardly acknowledges me as I hand it to him.

"Oh, thanks Mom," he replies nonchalantly and turns back to his friends.

Most of the decisions I agonize over don't deserve the anxiety I put into them.

For the deliberations of mortals are timid, /and unsure are our plans. Wis 9:14

Fearing the Worst

I sit in the doctor's office with a sick child on my lap. He's not interested in playing with any of the toys. He thumbs through the book he picked up with disinterest, then puts it down. He doesn't even ask me to read to him. I feel his forehead, pretending I'm just brushing his hair away. I don't want him to know I'm checking once again to see if his fever is gone.

My mind begins to imagine the worst. If I'm ready for the worst then it won't happen. Isn't that how it works? If I worry enough I can keep it from happening.

I imagine the valiant efforts of modern science to cure my son. I will focus my life around his possible illness. Whatever it takes, I will do.

I'm his mother.

His mother kept all these things in her heart.
Lk 2:51

Molds

Why can't people live and let live? Why can't they accept that no one can fill all their expectations? Why do they try to push others into their molds, and then blame them when they don't fit?

And why do we mothers pass on this legacy to our children?

———————————————

But by the grace of God I am what I am, and his grace to me has not been ineffective.
1 Cor 15:10

The Good Guys

"Don't shoot me, I'm a good guy," my four-year-old nephew shouts while playing "nasty boys"—their version of cops and robbers— with my sons.

If only life were so simple.

They don't know yet that good guys don't always win. That sometimes the good guys get shot. He doesn't remember the funeral for his father, a good cop who was killed before he was born.

Kids play cops and robbers in a world where good always overcomes evil. Unfortunately, real bad guys don't play by the rules of the game. They don't wear black and they don't know you aren't supposed to shoot the good guys.

How's a mother supposed to teach that?

Lord, show me your way; /lead me on a level path /because of my enemies. /Do not abandon me to the will of my foes; /malicious and lying witnesses have risen against me. Ps 27:11-12

Pain

Each day brings new pain from crippling arthritis. She fears the day when she'll no longer be able to walk. Sometimes she snaps at her daughter. Not because of anything the daughter has done, but because of what she represents. She is jealous of her daughter's youth.

The mother can't find the words to ask her daughter's forgiveness. She only snaps at her all the more.

Sometimes the mother sees the hurt in her daughter's eyes, struggling to understand her mother, to continue to love her.

That pain is worse than the arthritis.

If you, Lord, mark our sins, /Lord, who can stand? /But with you is forgiveness /and so you are revered. Ps 130:3-4

Miracle Child

Today they celebrated her fifth birthday, this child who fooled us all. From the very start she was no loser. She always came out on top, beating the odds. They said she wouldn't live to leave the hospital, but she showed them, coming home on her six-week birthday. Each day has brought her mother new delights.

The doctors say the little girl can't make it much longer, but her mother's counting on her to prove them wrong once again. And when her daughter finally does die, her mother will give thanks for every single day she was given with her beautiful child.

For each day has been a victory over death.

You formed my inmost being; /you knit me in my mother's womb. /I praise you, so wonderfully you made me; /wonderful are your works! /My very self you knew; /my bones were not hidden from you, /When I was being made in secret, /fashioned as in the depths of the earth. /Your eyes foresaw my actions; /in your book all are written down; /my days were shaped, before one came to be. Ps 139:15-16

Sitting Down to Eat

You mean meals were meant to be eaten sitting down? I had forgotten. Sure, I dream of a family that sits down together at supper time and has polite conversations.

But in the real world, my children breeze through, grab whatever there is to put in the microwave and gulp it down between a quick "Hi, Mom," and "Bye, Mom." And I grab a sandwich and kiss my husband good-bye as I pass him as he comes home from work and I head out to a PTA meeting.

It is a dream, this family that sits and eats meals together. Still, I can't shake this vague feeling that it could be true. That there will be a time—without club meetings, church events, athletic practices, music and ballet classes—when my family will sit down to eat.

He ordered the crowds to sit down on the grass. Taking the five loaves and the two fish, and looking up to heaven, he said the blessing, broke the loaves, and gave them to the disciples, who in turn gave them to the crowds. Mt 14:19

The Professional

She's a professional. She has all the degrees and letters after her name to prove it! People come to her for professional help. But sometimes she thinks that all her training and "expertise" has made her no better a mother. She looks at other mothers—the ones without degrees and training, who just naturally listen, the natural counselors—and feels that she's wasted a lifetime on her paper chase . . . only to become not more effective, but less effective, as a mother.

Her professional distance has gotten her just that—distance—from her own children. Her jargon, her professionalism, serves to separate her from them.

She's afraid that someday they are going to look behind the degrees and realize she's . . . a sham.

"But it shall not be so among you. Rather, whoever wishes to be great among you shall be your servant; whoever wishes to be first among you shall be your slave. Just so, the Son of Man did not come to be served but to serve and to give his life as a ransom for many."
Mt 20:26-28

The Room

The battle with my youngest son over the state of his room is one of the few constants in my life. It never ends.

We've lost many a search party in that room. His dad wandered lost for a week in the mess before finding his way out. Since then, no one else is allowed in the room unless connected to a lifeline.

My son doesn't seem bothered by the grunge. I plead, I threaten, I cajole him to clean his room. Afterwards, I find that all he has done is clean a path from the door to his bed.

It's not much, but it's progress.

You need endurance to do the will of God and receive what he has promised. Heb 10:36

Losing Battles

My children are fighters. If there's nothing to fight about, they manufacture something.

I, on the other hand, am pretty easygoing. I'm not overly set on having things a certain way. I'd gladly give in to my kids, if that would just satisfy them. But it doesn't.

So we battle, but they usually win.

I've heard there are children who bend naturally to their parent's will, who offer little or no resistance to authority. Can I put in an order for one?

For I will not dare to speak of anything except what Christ has accomplished through me to lead the Gentiles to obedience by word and deed, by the power of signs and wonders, by the power of the Spirit [of God]. Rom 15:18-19

> *Life in the Fast Lane*

Someday, I'll have more time—when I finish taking this class, when all the kids are in school, when they graduate, when I get this promotion or finish this degree or get a job with less hassles. Someday, I'll have time for all the things I want to do—for taking walks, reading books, watching mindless shows on TV, or star-gazing with my children.

Someday, I'll have more time, I say to myself. But then I realize that one class will lead to another class. The responsibilities of one job will give way to the responsibilities of a new job. The responsibilities of caring for pre-schoolers will give way to the responsibilities of raising school-aged children and then teenagers.

There will never be more time, unless I make that time now.

A thousand years in your eyes /are merely a yesterday. /But humans you return to dust, /saying, "Return, you mortals!" /Before a watch passes in the night, /you have brought them to their end; /They disappear like sleep at dawn; /they are like grass that dies. /It sprouts green in the morning; /by evening it is dry and withered. Ps 90:4-6

April 25

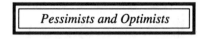

Pessimists and Optimists

I'm afraid my children are already pessimists. Every little disappointment is monumental, and every pleasure is minuscule—paling in contrast to the anticipation. A whole day of fun in the sun is forgotten when they are denied one last trip down the waterslide or one last ice cream cone. Rather than appreciating what they have, they bewail what they didn't get. The trip out for pizza becomes a disaster when the children at another table get a toy to take home and they don't.

I am now resigned to their pessimism and no longer let it bother me.

"You can sit here and cry all day, or you can get on with it, be happy with what you have, and have a good day. The choice is yours," I tell them. It's beginning to work.

Do you think I could raise a crop of optimists after all?

The plowman should plow in hope, and the thresher in hope of receiving a share. If we have sown spiritual seed for you, is it a great thing that we reap a material harvest from you?
1 Cor 9:10-11

Ideas of God

Our earliest ideas of God come from those closest to us as small children, often our mothers. If children are to grow spiritually, however, they need to evaluate those ideas. Just as they learn as they mature that their parents are not the all-powerful creatures they imagined them to be, they also need to realize that God doesn't have the same human failings and limitations their parents have.

God has many faces. God is mother/father/creator of all the world. God redeemed us through Jesus, God in human form. And God sustains us with a spirit that manifests itself as wind and fire. God is one and yet found in all creation. No single image of God can ever encompass the reality of God.

How can we mothers help our children know the incomprehensibility of God?

"I am the Alpha and the Omega," says the Lord God, "the one who is and who was and who is to come, the almighty." Rev 1:8

> *When I grow up. . .*

My kids think being an adult means doing what you please. No more parents to tell you what you can or cannot do. Stay up as late as you want, eat what you wish, watch whatever on TV.

The only problem is that adults have to come up with the money to buy the food, the TV, and the electricity. And somebody has to cook the food and wash the dishes. I guess I can stay up as late as I want. The only problem is that I have to pay for it in the morning. Get up, get the kids to school, fix their lunches, clean the house . . .

Being an adult is not all it is cracked up to be.

God, you have taught me from my youth; /to this day I proclaim your wondrous deeds. /Now that I am old and gray, /do not forsake me, God, /that I may proclaim your might /to all generations yet to come. Ps 71:17-18

Family Stories

Grandmother takes the small hands into hers, one child on either side, and together they all walk to the park. She watches as they throw bread crumbs to the ducks and giggle and shriek as the ducks approach too close for their comfort. She pushes them on the swings, just as she did their father before them. She finally gets them to leave, coaxed by the promise of ice cream. She tells them stories of how it was when their dad was little.

Wide-eyed, and with smiles of disbelief, they laugh at her stories. It doesn't seem possible to them that their father was ever their age. It doesn't seem possible to her either, and yet it's true. Such a short time ago he sat at her kitchen table and told her about his day. Now his children sit in his place. It won't be long before they have children of their own. Then they will pass on her family's stories to their children and to their children's children.

Since many have undertaken to compile a narrative of the events that have been fulfilled among us, just as those who were eyewitnesses from the beginning and ministers of the word have handed them down to us, I too have decided, after investigating everything accurately anew, to write it down in an orderly sequence for you, most excellent Theophilus, so that you may realize the certainty of the teachings you have received. Lk 1:1-3

Stray Dogs

"Mommy!" They run screaming into the house. "There's a dog chasing us," my daughter and her friend shout. They are crying and shaking. I chase the dog out of the yard and assure them it's OK. They don't believe me. They stay in the house and refuse to go out.

I'm furious. My child has a right to play in her own yard with her friends without fear of dogs running loose in the neighborhood. Nor should women have to fear driving places at night. And old people should not have to be afraid to go out of their homes in broad daylight.

There's something wrong with a world where people live in fear. I can try to help my daughter overcome her fear of strange dogs. I can teach her how to handle them, how to protect herself, what to watch out for. When she's older I can teach her what streets to avoid, how to defend herself if she's attacked, ways to protect herself from becoming a victim.

But I shouldn't have to!

Watch carefully then how you live, not as foolish persons but as wise, making the most of the opportunity, because the days are evil.
Eph 5:15-16

Bubbles

A cry is heard from the back porch where my son has just gone to blow bubbles. I rush out to discover the catastrophe—spilled bubble stuff his kindergarten teacher had given him for Christmas.

"There's still some in the bottle," I reassure him.

"I know, but it was a present from Miss Densmore," he sobs.

I comfort him and dry his tears. We stand out on the porch blowing bubbles, watching them float—multi-colored transparent balls blowing gently on the wind. We try to catch them, with no luck. One touch and they disappear. He talks about school, what he's learning, his current passions. And we watch another bubble blow off in the breeze. The bubbles don't break right away when they land on the jagged grass, yet do when they land on our smooth hands. We blow giant bubbles and tiny bubbles and watch them settle in the yard.

A few bubbles remain on the grass, but not for long.

Like a ship traversing the heaving water, /of which, when it has passed, no trace can be found, /no path of its keel in the waves.
Wis 5:10

> ### Mud Puddle Jumping

The temptation is too great. I can see it in his young face. The desire to run and jump and splash is offset by the scolding he knows he'll get if he comes in covered with mud. He pauses, does a little dance, side-steps the puddle. But then some kids ride by on bikes through the puddles, raising their own feet to avoid the water, but splashing my son.

He pauses a moment more. Then, realizing the die is cast, he jumps in shoes and all. Watching from the house, I groan, but resist the urge to scream as I observe his youthful abandon . . . not careless, but carefree.

I give him this moment to himself to savor, to bask in the wonderfulness of youth, to forget—if only for a while—the responsibilities of growing up.

When do mothers lose the ability to jump—shoes on—into mud puddles?

———————————————

*Rejoice, O young man, while you are young
/and let your heart be glad in the days of your
youth. /Follow the ways of your heart, /the
vision of your eyes; /yet understand that as
regards all this /God will bring you to judge-
ment. /Ward off grief from your heart
/and put away trouble from your presence,
/though the dawn of youth is fleeting.
Eccl 11:9-10*

Life at the Top

The first time she was invited to a "high-level" meeting where the big deals are really done, she thought she had made it.

That was ten years ago. The world today looks much the same as it did then. So little has changed. She used to relish being the only woman in men-only gatherings, now she feels the strain of it. Sometimes she wants to break out, but she knows that to do so, to miss one of those cocktail parties, may mean missing the deal of her life. Still, she longs to stay at home and soak in the tub and play with her children.

Life at the top, for mothers, is still a mixed bag.

But according to his promise we await new heavens and a new earth in which righteousness dwells. 2 Pt 3:13

Exclusivity

"Mommy, we want you all to ourselves," my daughters inform me as I push them on swings. They suspiciously eye the other children entering the park, watching lest they, too, want me to play with them.

Kids want to possess their parents. To have adults at their exclusive beck and call gives them a sense of power, however unreal, that their small developing egos need.

Adults, likewise, often seek an exclusive relationship with God. Childishly, we try to define whom God is to love; whom to help. We try to control the all-powerful God so that we too have a sense of power, however unreal, that our small egos need.

Just as our children need to learn that they are not in charge and that Mom and Dad's love can extend beyond their immediate family, so adults need to learn and accept that it is not we who are in charge, but God, and that God's love goes where God pleases.

But when the kindness and generous love /of God our savior appeared, /not because of any righteous deeds we had done /but because of his mercy, /he saved us through the bath of rebirth /and renewal by the Holy Spirit. Ti 3:4-5

On Being Human

Can I forgive my mother for not being perfect?
For not living up to my child-like imaginings? In my
eyes she was all goodness and light, yet all darkness
each time she thwarted my young will.

I tried to split that dark side of her off, deny it
existed, see only the goodness and light. But the
darkness still remained. It claimed its rightful place
alongside her good side, and I found that it wasn't so
bad. Her dark one wasn't evil, but a hurt, grieving
child, scared to come out. And the light side wasn't all
good. Sometimes it was a self-righteous, cold piety
that lacked human depth.

And so I discovered that my mother was human.
Can I forgive her for being less than a goddess? Will
my children be able to forgive me some day?

---

*"Stop judging that you may not be judged. For
as you judge, so will you be judged, and the
measure with which you measure will be
measured out to you."* Mt 7:1-2

Dandelions

"What are you doing?" my daughter asks.

"Pulling dandelions," I respond.

"Oh," she pauses, "I like dandelions. I think they're pretty. I like it when I see whole fields of yellow in the sun."

"But they're weeds," I point out rationally.

She says nothing else as I furiously, stubbornly, work away. She appears bemused by my fervent attack.

I finally give in, admit defeat, and let the dandelions win another round. One month later, they are all gone, having naturally lived out their function.

Maybe it's time I learned to love dandelions.

For see, the winter is past, /the rains are over and gone. /The flowers appear on the earth, /the time of pruning the vines has come, /and the song of the dove is heard in our land.
Song 2:11-12

Non-Violence

It was easy for Jesus to be non-violent—he wasn't a mother! He didn't have his four-year-old son sticking out his tongue at him while he delivered the Sermon on the Mount. He never experienced his three-year-old twins use his new tunic as a napkin. He never had to drag a five-year-old kicking and screaming out of the synagogue, every eye on him.

I also find it hard to believe that Jesus, being a normal, healthy boy, didn't try his mother's patience with childish antics. That he never resisted going to bed at night and always ate everything on his plate. Nor that Mary, being a Jewish mother of that day and age, never scolded her son, never found herself at cross purposes with him, and always spared the rod.

Non-violence is easy . . . if you're not a mother.

When his parents saw him, they were aston-ished, and his mother said to him, "Son, why have you done this to us?" Lk 2:48

Envy

Envy, that green-eyed monster, is lurking around the corner. Beware.

It causes children to fight. It creates competition. It destroys friendships. And it isn't something we outgrow. Rather it grows with us and becomes more terrible and fierce with the passing years—unless we learn to tame this fierce beast.

Envy leads mothers to strike out at others, to criticize and complain, to drag others down rather than rejoicing with them. It makes us quick to find fault and pick fights, quicker even than our children.

Envy is a deceptive creature that grows more cunning daily. It poses as "constructive" criticism or self-righteous indignation. It eats at us because we are insecure and unhappy with ourselves and our own accomplishments.

Like children fighting over whom Mom likes best, we focus on what we don't have that others do, and fail to recognize the Creator's equal love for all.

Envy and anger shorten one's life, /worry brings on premature old age. Sir 30:24

Family Heirlooms

"What do we need with more dishes?" my husband complains as I unpack the box of treasures. "We've hardly enough room for all the dishes we already have."

He doesn't understand. These chipped, mismatched dishes are my childhood. The cookie jar Grandma filled with sugar cookies, the big roaster in which Mom made our Sunday pot roast—remnants of a childhood long ago, almost forgotten. Memories of good times and bad times at the dinner table, of learning how to cook. The time I forgot to add the baking powder to the cake. The day I burned the chicken. The lumpy mashed potatoes.

Cereal bowls, mismatched but sturdy so they wouldn't break when washed by young hands. Chipped plates, banged countless times against the sink. Odds and ends that make a funny, incongruous whole. But that whole is me: chipped and broken and glued back together, hardened and bent from years in and out of the oven, filled with the bitter and the sweet.

May the eyes of [your] hearts be enlightened,
that you may know what is the hope that
belongs to his call, what are the riches of glory
in his inheritance among the holy ones, and
what is the surpassing greatness of his power
for us who believe, in accord with the exercise
of his great might. Eph 1:18-19

Competition

The young men swarm around her daughters like bees to honey. They sit on the porch and talk every afternoon. She invites them in for a snack and thinks, "am I still attractive in these boys' eyes?"

She's ashamed even as she thinks this. What is she doing? These are her daughters' boyfriends. How can she compete with a sixteen-year-old and seventeen-year-old? Why would she want to?

She can still turn a head or two when she walks down the street. In fact, sexually, she's in her prime. There's something to be said for being a more mature woman.

She'll never be a teenager again, thank God. Still the urge to compete with her daughters remains.

Charm is deceptive and beauty fleeting; /the woman who fears the LORD is to be praised. /Give her a reward of her labors, /and let her works praise her at the city gates.
Prv 31:30-31

Gardening

Gardening is a miracle. You drop a seed into the ground, and it grows. I don't know the first thing about gardening, and yet my garden still thrives. What's more, my children—who know even less than I and who throw all their seeds together in a handful of clumps—are also growing things.

We don't have degrees in agriculture or horticulture, yet we can still grow a garden—much to God's merit rather than our own. Even if we could predict the weather and knew the most favorable growing times, it wouldn't guarantee that we'd do any better than we do now.

Such is God's dominion.

It is the same with kids. Mothers don't need a degree in biology or gynecology to have a baby. We can stop the growth or we can help it along, but there's nothing we can do to guarantee a good crop.

That rests, ultimately, in the hands of the Almighty.

In the morning sow your seed, /and at evening let not your hand be idle; /for you know not which of the two will be successful, /or whether both alike will turn out well. Eccl 11:6

The Planet Called Childhood

My children live in their own little world. It's as foreign to me as another planet. It's the planet called childhood. I visited it once, many years ago. The memories are so dim now, clouded over in illusions. I can hardly separate the wheat from the chaff. Were the years really as good as I want to believe? Were they really as bad as I sometimes fear?

Sometimes I wonder how my children will remember their childhood. Will they recall the good times more than the bad? Will they cherish the trips to the zoo and stopping for ice cream or try to repress the arguments over homework and a messy house?

Will their memories be more sweet than sour? Whatever they are, they will be memories of a time and a space and a world I no longer inhabit.

At that very moment he rejoiced [in] the holy Spirit and said, "I give you praise, Father, Lord of heaven and earth, for although you have hidden these things from the wise and the learned you have revealed them to the childlike." Lk 10:21

Trust

Lying awake, worrying. Waiting for the sounds of a car door slamming shut, steps on the porch, and the back door opening.

Why did I say she could go to the concert? I knew I had a busy day tomorrow and I need my sleep, but I can't get it for worrying. Will she be all right driving all that way? Will she pay attention to the road ahead of her or be diverted by her friend's chatter? And even if she's alert, what about the other drivers on the road? I guess its better that she's driving, rather than someone else. My daughter is reliable and a good driver. Still, I can't get to sleep.

I get up, go downstairs, and look out the front window . . . only to make a mad dash for the bedroom as her car drives in. Can't let her know how worried I was! She'd say I didn't trust her!

I hear her footsteps on the porch, the back door slam, the refrigerator door open and close. I roll over, utter a prayer of thanksgiving, and fall asleep.

---

*"O LORD, my rock, my fortress, my deliverer,
/my God, my rock of refuge! /My shield, the
horn of my salvation, /my stronghold, my refuge,
/my savior, from violence you keep me safe.
/'Praised be the LORD,' I exclaim, /and I am
safe from my enemies." 2 Sam 22:2-4*

Heaven

She pins the last curler in place and adds the magic solution that makes straight hair curly, then sits, allowing the chemicals to do their work. Her stomach is large in front of her, her feet aching. The smells of the different solutions no longer make her nauseous as they did during her first months, but the long hours on her feet get increasingly difficult as her pregnancy wears on and her girth widens. If only she could afford to quit. But the lost wages from the earlier months were hard enough. She must save every penny, every hour of vacation time and sick leave in order to have time with her newborn baby.

Maybe it will be a girl. She'll curl the child's hair and braid ribbons in it. She is always fixing a stranger's hair. Wouldn't it be heaven if all she had to do was fix her own daughter's?

While they were looking intently at the sky as he was going, suddenly two men dressed in white garments stood beside them. They said, "Men of Galilee, why are you standing there looking at the sky? This Jesus who has been taken up from you in heaven will return in the same way as you have seen him going into heaven."
Acts 1:10-11

Just a Kid

"Don't blame me. I'm just a little kid."

How true, dear child, how true. You are just a little kid.

How I long to say the same words: "Don't blame me, I'm still a little kid." I may give the appearance of being grown up. The gray in my hair announces I'm getting older, but inside I'm still too young and inexperienced to be a mother. I don't know what I'm doing half the time. I try to rely on my "maternal instinct" to help me raise my children, only to be warned by experts to suspect those very instincts. I fear making the same mistakes my own mother—who implanted those instincts in me—made.

So I fumble around and do my best. I'm still too young to carry such responsibility, yet carry it I must.

When I was a child, I used to talk as a child, think as a child, reason as a child; when I became a man, I put aside childish things. At present we see indistinctly, as in a mirror, but then face to face. At present I know partially; then I shall know fully, as I am fully known.
1 Cor 13:11-12

> *Grandma*

Her baby just had a baby. It's too wonderful to be true. It's too awful to be true. She can't be that old. A grandmother? It's just not possible. She remembers too well when her daughter was born, pink and wrinkled, eyes tightly shut. Now those eyes are gazing upon her own child.

She had fought back the urge to rush to the hospital the minute she heard her child was in labor. This time was for her daughter and her husband. She tried not to pace or think too much about it. She remembered other trips to the hospital, waiting while her daughter's appendix was removed, waiting while the doctor set her broken arm after the tumble on the ice. She thought about that night, so many years ago, when this bundle of trouble and joy had burst into her life.

Now she could be contained no longer.

"I'll be right there," she says and hangs up. She rushes to the hospital, anxiously attending the ticking of the clock until visiting hours begin and she can see her granddaughter.

Her baby had a baby!

---

*I recall your sincere faith that first lived in your
grandmother Lois and in your mother Eunice
and that I am confident lives also in you.*
2 Tm 1:5

The Incredible Expanding Mother

I'll never be a size eight again. Right now I'd settle for a ten or even a matronly twelve. Anything besides this balloon I call a body.

By me walk all these svelte blonds and brunettes with long legs and slender waists. What do I get for the honor of pregnancy? The body of a beached whale. I waddle to the closest ice cream store and console myself with a double dip chocolate, with chocolate fudge and macadamia nuts.

Walking past the hard-bodied career women are the matronly women with two or three kids in tow. I see my future in their gait. Weighed down by diaper bags and boxes of graham crackers, they gaze longingly at the manikins in the dress store windows, only to press on to the nearest K-Mart or Woolworth's to buy children's socks on special.

But then I'm surprised as one of the matrons with three kids in tow is joined by a beautiful, thin red-head. One of the three runs to her and throws her arms around her "Momma."

I pat my belly. I *can* be a size eight again.

---

*"Amen, I say to you, if you have faith the size of
a mustard seed, you will say to this mountain,
'move from here to there,' and it will move.
Nothing will be impossible for you."*
Mt 17:20-21

Life Goes On

Something is wrong. She knows it. This is more than the usual trials of life with a teenager, more than the moodiness of disappointments in romance and failing to make cheerleader. Something is really wrong.

Her daughter is pregnant.

"Oh, Mom, I'm so ashamed."

What does she say to her? Life must go on. Mother and daughter hug each other in their mutual pain.

And then they make plans. The daughter will keep the baby. The mother will go to Lamaze classes with her. Grandmother will help raise her grandchild until daughter is able to raise the child on her own.

Now is not the time to wallow in shame or indulge in feelings of failure.

Life goes on.

Lord, do not withhold your compassion from me; /may your enduring kindness ever preserve me. Ps 40:12

The Guilties

I suffer from a dreadful, life-threatening disease—the Guilties. The Guilties come in many forms: Catholic Guilties, white Guilties, middle-class Guilties, working mother Guilties. I've had them all. They arise at a moment's notice and incapacitate me or trap me into doing things.

Having lived with this disease for most of my adult life, I have come to the conclusion that—much like the alcoholic—I am powerless before this illness. The very effort to rid my life of all the "shoulds" ends up being yet another "should." Yet, left untreated, this disease can rob us of the joy we were created to experience. It can turn life into a heavy burden to be endured, rather than a wonder to be experienced. It can rob us of the joy of giving spontaneously and freely. It can keep us from living the abundant life God promises us.

Alone, there is nothing we addicts can do to cure the Guilties. The power of this disease is such that we can convince ourselves that we really want to do what our guilt has put us up to. In order to escape its clutches, we need each other. Maybe I should start a support group for those suffering from the Guilties.

There I go again.

We have all withered like leaves, /and our guilt carries us away like the wind. Is 64:5

> ### Solomon

"Blessed are they who know their kid's needs, for they shall be filled."

How's that for a new addition to the Beatitudes? How simple . . . and yet so difficult.

My children's desires are many. They want a new doll or a new bike, this outfit or that game. They may even tell me they "need" it. How hard it is for a mother to make the distinction. The dress my daughter "needs" may be an unnecessary luxury, or it may very well be critical to her feeling of self-esteem.

A mother needs the wisdom of Solomon.

I do as you requested. I give you a heart so wise and understanding that there has never been anyone like you up to now, and after you there will come no one to equal you. 1 Kgs 3:12

> *Grace*

"Where are you going?" the sales clerk questions the woman in front of me.

"Away. All by myself!"

"Who'll be watching your kids? Grandparents?"

"No, my husband is taking a few days off. It's his birthday gift to me, a long weekend alone to do whatever I want."

What a treat! Time to think, to play, to pray— *sans* children, *sans* spouse.

I watch the woman leave the store. There, but for the lack of grace of my husband, go I.

You husbands should live with your wives in understanding. 1 Pt 3:7

> **Breasts**

"You need to have a mammogram," the doctor tells her. Distracted, she makes an appointment for the test, then waits and worries.

Why the breasts? Why not something—anything—else? Five years ago, she had had a Pap test come back abnormal. That didn't bother her as much as this. Take out the uterus. She's through bearing kids. What does she need it for anymore? But her breasts are a visible sign of her womanliness.

Her husband reassures her. It doesn't matter to him he says. But does he really mean it? They gave him so much pleasure in the past.

They bring her pleasure, too.

I am a wall, /and my breasts are like towers. /So now in his eyes I have become /one to be welcomed. Song 8:10

Trusting God

It's not that I don't trust you, God. It's just that I know all too well where that trust has led me in the past! I've always made it through the situations you've gotten me into, but that doesn't mean it's been easy or without pain.

I wish trusting you meant nothing serious would ever happen to my family—no life-threatening illnesses, no accidents, no financial crises, no marital difficulties, no problems with kids. We both know that's not the way it works. We believers are just as prone to the tragedies of everyday life as anyone else.

Trust you? I have no choice. I will not get out of this world alive, but at least when I go I'll have you by my side.

———————————————

"Master, to whom shall we go? You have the words of eternal life." Jn 6:68

Truth or Consequences

"Truth or consequences." What a misleading phrase! It implies that if you tell the truth you can escape the consequences of your actions.

Maybe "truth *and* consequences" would be a better saying, but then who would want to tell the truth?

My son is under the mistaken impression that as long as he owns up and apologizes for something he should get off scot-free. I try to explain to him that there have to be consequences for his actions and that saying he is sorry does not mean he will not pay them. So then, he figures, why tell the truth at all? I point out that I go easier on him when he tells the truth and apologizes than when he lies. We go around and around about it.

Perhaps it should be "truth and (but not as bad as without the truth) consequences."

Truth will spring from the earth, /justice will look down from heaven. Ps 85:12

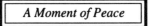

A Moment of Peace

I wake up at the usual time, but everyone else is still asleep. This is it, I think. This may very well be my chance. If I get up now, maybe I'll be able to have a cup of coffee in peace.

Part of me says I'm a fool. Better to stay in bed and get what peace I can lying there. My children have radar, especially on Saturdays. They know the minute I step foot out of bed. But we let them stay up late last night. Just maybe today they'll sleep in.

I slip out of bed, quietly reach for my bathrobe, and tip-toe down the carpeted stairs. I don't even close the bedroom door behind me to allow my husband to sleep, lest the kids hear me. This is every person for him or her self! I make it to the kitchen, pour the water in the coffee pot, only to hear from the family room, "When's breakfast, Mom?"

"Peace, peace!" they say, /though there is no peace. Jer 6:14

Blindness

There are many forms of blindness. Not all are bad. To be blind to the small faults of a spouse—a blessing! To overlook a few forgotten clothes strewn on the floor by a child in a moment of haste—a blessing! To know when to see and when not to see, when to correct and when to let slide—a blessing!

There is also a blindness that kills. Being blind to injustice, blind to a hurting child crying out for attention, blind to our own faults that protrude like beams in our eyes or warts on our flesh–such is deadly, deathly blindness.

The blindness that is a blessing sees all that is necessary and nothing that is superfluous. The blindness that brings death is a mask of denial that sees only the trivially unimportant, and even that in a warped way.

Sight has more to do with the mind than with the eye.

"If you were blind, you would have no sin; but now you are saying, 'We see,' so your sin remains." Jn 9:41

Adventures

I'm not one for adventures. They upset my eating and sleeping habits. I like my day neatly planned and organized and wrapped in cellophane. But then the greatest adventure of all, this baby child, came along and ripped through my packaging. I haven't had a decent meal or a good night's sleep since!

I've been told that children thrive on having a consistent schedule, but I've yet to figure out what schedule this child is on. Maybe this one's scheduled around her whim: to wake at three ready to eat, or to cry for an hour first; to nap for three hours in the afternoon, or to fuss until suppertime and then fall asleep.

Still, now that I've stumbled off on this adventure—albeit awkwardly—I'm finding there are worse things in life than an upset eating schedule or disrupted sleep patterns.

Israel set out with all that was his. Gn 46:1

Stories

My son and I have a game we used to play while driving to and from day-care. It's called Puff. Somehow we started making up stories around this mythical character Puff, the magic dragon. Puff would take my son and his friends to enchanted lands and far away places, backward and forward in time. Depending on his latest fascination, my son and Puff would fight fires, bust ghosts, and—most recently—live down in the sewer and battle bad guys while scarfing down a few pizzas.

I must say that none of these stories were great inspirations. At 7:45 A.M., my head was usually too preoccupied with what I needed to do that day to give too much thought to being creative. Still, between the two of us, my son and I managed to piece together some things remotely resembling actual stories. At his promptings this game went on for about two years, so I guess maybe the important part wasn't so much the content as that we did it together.

Mothers and children may not be master storytellers, but love will forgive a thousand literary errors.

I will open my mouth in story, /drawing lessons from of old. /We have heard them, we know them; /our ancestors have recited them to us. /We do not keep them from our children; /we recite them to the next generation. Ps 78:2-4

Relief Pitcher

I've never been that great a fan of baseball, but now that my son is in little league I've been compelled to learn the game.

One aspect of the sport I've come to admire is how the coach sends in a relief pitcher for one who's having a bad day or is just tired out. It's such a simple concept that makes so much sense.

Why can't we mothers call in a relief pitcher more often? Why can't we ask our husbands to take over when we are having a bad day? And when our husbands are too tired why can't babysitters and grandparents come in from the bullpen? Sound simple? Then why don't we do it more often? Why do we mothers refuse to seek necessary relief from our kids! Why do we continue to keep pitching, even when we are throwing wildly into the grandstand?

If only we had an understanding coach who would pull us out of the game. But then, nobody wants to "grab some bench."

———————————

Gracious is the LORD and just; /yes, our God is merciful. /The LORD protects the simple; /I was helpless, but God saved me. /Return, my soul, to your rest; /the LORD has been good to you.
Ps 116:5-7

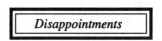

Disappointments

My daughter just learned a hard lesson. The best person doesn't always win. Life isn't always fair.

What do I say to her? That it really doesn't matter? That there are plenty of cheerleaders who never amount to anything in the adult world? That ten years from now it won't matter? But she'll still feel her loss. Surely there's always next year and another chance, but there will not be another chance this year.

The fact is, sometimes the best person doesn't win. Sometimes the best candidate loses. Sometimes the most qualified job applicant is passed over for someone with the "right" connections.

Even if we don't really want to enter a room, it still hurts when the door is slammed in our face.

Is it in vain I have kept my heart clean /washed my hands in innocence? /For I am afflicted day after day, /chastised every morning. Ps 73:13-14.

Bikes

Up and down hills, side streets and alleyways. Such fond memories I have of riding bikes: the wind in my face, a feeling of glee and freedom running through my veins, independence—if only for a short time.

That was before the days of ten-speeds and bike helmets. No one worried about such things. There was only one speed to be had. No one wore a helmet. We rode bikes alone, in pairs, in groups with wild abandon.

Now my son takes off on his bike. I see the same glow of freedom, the same burst of independence, but now I worry. I run beside my daughter, helping her learn to ride. Yet the minute I let go and she's on her own, I am afraid. Will they watch out for cars? Will they go too fast and take a tumble? I invest in all types of safety gear—helmets, knee pads, elbow pads—all spurned by my children for making them look like nerds.

They take off around the corner with their friends.

Some day, they'll be driving cars.

They shall eat bread which they have weighed out anxiously, and they shall drink water which they have weighed out fearfully. Ez 4:16

Community

It takes a community to raise a child. No mother alone can do it. Not even two parents can expect to have any success. It takes aunts and uncles, grandmas and grandpas, the people next door and down the street, the teachers at school, the preacher at church, the grocer, the baker, the police officer, the firefighter, the librarian, the babysitter . . . .

It takes a community to raise a child. Mothers cannot do it alone because we were not meant to do it alone. No matter how we may try to isolate ourselves, we cannot avoid being affected by the community we live in, and in turn having an affect on that community.

Thank you to all the people who have helped and will help to raise my children. I'll try to do the same for you and yours.

They devoted themselves to the teaching of the apostles and to the communal life, to the breaking of the bread and to the prayers.
Acts 2:42

Firefighters

The heat blazes around her as she approaches the smoking building. The rescue team has already entered to search for any victims. They've been told there may be someone at home, a child. She waits, part of the fire fighting crew, ready to enter in a moment if necessary. Her face mask is tight against her face. The heat of the heavy gear on this hot night already causes trickles of sweat to pour down her forehead. The rescuers come out carrying a small body, limp but still alive.

The firefighters go in, crawling on their knees and breathing heavily through their Scott packs, crawling through the smoking rooms. They search for the seat of the fire to make a direct attack, realizing they have already lost precious moments. The air sirens sound and they are ordered out immediately. The fire is spreading too rapidly for them to contain.

Outside, other firefighters are using hoseline on the flames shooting out the top. She turns and breathes a sign of relief. Not for herself, but for the child . . . and for her own.

He rescued us from such great danger of death, and he will continue to rescue us; in him we have put our hope [that] he will also rescue us again. 2 Cor 1:10

Non-Renewable Commodities

Time. Energy. Life.

In a throw-away society where we are encouraged to go out and spend, spend, spend, buy, buy, buy, some things are non-renewable. No matter how much money we have, we cannot add a single minute extra to our day. No riches can buy us more energy once we've run out. And nothing in the material realm can bring back a life once gone.

In a world that advises us to shop till we drop, is it possible for mothers to start focusing on those non-renewable commodities?

Time. Energy. Life.

Far better to throw away money than any of these.

_____

Watch carefully then how you live, not as foolish persons but as wise, making the most of the opportunity, because the days are evil.
Eph 5:15-16

One at a Time

There is constant noise in my house. Everybody talks at the same time, and somehow I'm supposed to be able to hear them and respond to all their questions and demands.

"One at a time, one at a time," I keep repeating, to little avail.

God can hear all of us all the time, of course. Somehow God makes sense out of all the uproar and commotion. If we mothers are to listen to God, however, we need to give God some undivided attention.

As hard as it is to listen to our children when they all talk at once, it's even harder to listen to God amidst all the noise and distraction. Somehow we have to find quiet time to hear God.

"May your ear be attentive, and your eyes open, to heed the prayer which I, your servant, now offer in your presence." Neh 1:6

A Companion

A rabbit appears before her, nibbling the long grass, oblivious to her presence. It skips amidst the tombstones, and she feels strangely less alone.

Her beautiful, golden-haired boy is gone, but she visits his grave after all these years. There is still an ache within her, a spot where her son lives. She trims the grass around his grave and places a pot of flowers by his name.

For all her pain, she wouldn't give up one moment of his precious years on this earth. Like the rabbit, he made her feel less alone.

See, I am sending an angel before you, to guard you on the way and bring you to the place I have prepared. Ex 23:20

Leave a Message

Some people hate answering machines. I love them. They're a way of letting the people I care about know I am thinking about them, even when they are not available.

Notes and letters used to serve this purpose. People got their mail, even if they were gone for a while. The mail waited for them. Now people get messages on their machines. What a wonderful invention for our busy times!

Nor do I worry about the bleeps with no answer afterward indicating that someone had called me and not left a message. That's their choice. They can call back. I can't always be at home waiting for a possible call. And sometimes I choose to be at home but unavailable, and the answering machine gives me the ability to do that. It puts a little control back in my life.

We have no God-like ability to be available to everyone twenty-four hours a day. So leave a message.

Then when all his attendents had left his presence, and Ehud went in to him where he sat alone in his cool upper room, Ehud said, "I have a message from God for you."
Jgs 3:19-20

The Wedding

I sit in the back of church at my friend's wedding, my newborn nestled on my shoulder, my four-year-old squirming at my side. My husband is in the wedding party. He's handsome in his grey tux. I remember another wedding several years ago, my own. How handsome my husband was then. How nervous I was. The years have changed us, but not that much. The laughs have sustained us through the tears. Here we are, still together, more committed to each other than ever, more in love than ever.

I glance at my husband and remember. We're not that different from how we were then—him a little heavier, a little balder; me with stretch marks and the hint of gray hair.

We go to the reception, toast the bride and groom, and dance. The past years fade away, the future is distant, and we are lost in the present—lost and in love.

Though the mountains leave their place and the hills be shaken, /My love shall never leave you /nor my covenant of peace be shaken, /says the LORD, who has mercy on you. Is 54:10

| *One-Minute Vacations* |

Vacation time is upon us. While part of me still longs for trips to exotic places or extended lengths of time away at a cottage, the appeal of these vacations lessens when children are added to the equation. They require so much extra luggage and so much entertaining when removed from their natural habitat. The best vacations can be taken year round on a daily basis. They don't cost a penny or require elaborate preparations, and they leave you feeling rejuvenated and ready to deal with the rest of the day.

These are the one-minute vacations that can catch you unaware. They are those moments when all the children are playing quietly together or taking naps and the phone isn't ringing. They are the opportunities when you can sit down and just relax and enjoy the beauty of the day. They are the times when you make an appointment with yourself which is just as important as all the other appointments in your life.

I've learned to vacation at home all year long. All it requires is the ability to seize the moment; to see the potential rest in any given day and use it; to not be afraid to waste time on yourself.

"I, myself," the LORD answered, "will go along, to give you rest." Ex 33:14

Hanging Clothes

I always had to help my mom with the laundry when I was little. I remember watching as she sent clothes through the wringer washer, checking to make sure none of them got stuck and started going round and round rather than through and out, fearing lest my fingers get caught and squeezed in the contraption despite Mom's repeated assurances that it couldn't happen from my side.

Later, I would stand outside under the clothes-line, handing clothes and clothespins to my mother and—once I was tall enough—hanging the clothes myself.

Now I have a home of my own and my own automatic washer and dryer. But still, on warm summer days, I go outside with wet laundry first thing in the morning while the grass is still wet with dew and hang the clothes on the line. I pause to note the clear blue sky. I listen to the birds and feel the breeze. I take my time.

It brings back memories of my childhood . . . and Mom.

"Do this in remembrance of me." 1 Cor 11:24

Chocolate in the morning,

Chocolate in the noontime,

Chocolate at supper time,

Just give me some chocolate,

and I don't care what kind!

Let me lie in a bed of chocolate euphoria. Worries and cares are drowned in a whirl of chocolate. Popping M&Ms once the kids are in school. Sneaking bits of chocolate almond candy bars behind the bathroom door. And the ultimate delight, Chocolate Peanut Butter Cup Ice Cream, once my children are safely nestled in bed!

Who said being pregnant couldn't be fun?

The disciples of John and of the Pharisees were accustomed to fast. People came to him and objected. "Why do the disciples of John and the disciples of the Pharisees fast, but your disciples do not fast?" Jesus answered them, "Can the wedding guests fast while the bridegroom is with them? As long as they have the bridegroom with them they cannot fast." Mk 2:18-19

Bats in the Belfry

I'm awakened by the sudden jump of my husband and the sound of wings. "There's a bat in here," he says.

We instinctively cover our heads with the covers and hide while we reconnoiter. The bat flies out of our room and we're momentarily relieved, only to realize it could have gone into our daughter's room. We jump out of bed, ready to risk our lives to defend our child.

Our little girl is sitting up in bed, wondering what is going on. "Its just a bat," I tell her, "go back to sleep. We'll take care of it." I shut her door to keep the bat out.

Armed with a broom and a towel, my husband and I stand ready, baseball caps covering our heads. Every light in the house is on as we open the front door. The bat swoops around our house for a while in a circling pattern, until it finally finds the open door and escapes.

Aren't most of our fears like that bat? When confronted by the light, they disappear.

"Therefore do not be afraid of them. Nothing is concealed that will not be revealed, nor secret that will not be known." Mt 10:26

Transitions

It happens every summer. The transition from the kids' going to school to being home for summer vacation is very messy. New structures need to be set up, new routines established. It takes time before we all settle in. In the process, the kids and I are usually at each other's throats.

The same thing happens with any transition in a family. Dad's long awaited promotion to a new job brings benefits, but also tensions. It takes awhile for the whole family to get used to his new schedule. When Mom returns to work after being home with the kids, it takes time for everyone to adjust.

Funny, I don't remember it being that way as a child. I don't remember any big traumas associated with these events. Why is it I see them so clearly now?

Maybe it's the moms, not the children, who need help with the transitions.

No trial has come to you but what is human. God is faithful and will not let you be tried beyond your strength; but with the trial he will also provide a way out, so that you may be able to bear it. 1 Cor 10:13

Thunderstorms

I thought, "Maybe they won't wake up." But no, the next thunder clap was followed by a chorus of frightened "Mom's!" and three figures appearing at my bedroom doorway.

"It's all right," I reassure them. "It's just the angels bowling."

"But why do they have to be so loud?" my son asks.

"Because during the day they're so busy watching over us, at night they need to have some fun," I explain lamely.

They stay with me until the storm moves on and only a low grumble in the distance remains.

I don't want my children to fear the majesty of the storm, and so I must be strong and without fear.

The voice of the LORD is over the waters; /the God of glory thunders, /the LORD, over the mighty waters. /The voice of the LORD is power, /the voice of the LORD is splendor. Ps 29:3-4

> Safety

In and out my kids run, followed by any number of neighborhood children. They appear suddenly in my yard, then disappear to the next. It's nice to live in a neighborhood where children run as freely in your neighbor's backyard as in your own.

And yet, even here there is a need for caution. A need to watch out. Even in the best of neighborhoods, children are kidnapped or abused. No place is completely secure. No one is completely safe from harm.

The only true security lies in a God who loves us. Sometimes even that can be hard to hold on to in a world such as ours. Yet we mothers must strive to give our children the greatest security we have—the belief in a God who is good and loving.

Therefore, put on the armor of God, that you may be able to resist on the evil day and, having done everything, to hold your ground. Eph 6:13

Clean House

The children are playing in the mud while I do their laundry! Inside me there is a battle raging between the child in me who longs to build forts in the woods with my children and the adult who wants a clean house and clothes. (After all, our environment does shape us. Living in a dirty, cluttered house leads to a messy, cluttered mind. Doesn't it?)

I want light and air to fill my house—not a spotless spic and span, but an uncluttered atmosphere that is simple and ready to respond to God at a moment's notice.

"What woman having ten coins and losing one would not light a lamp and sweep the house, searching carefully until she finds it?" Lk 15:8

> **Abundance**

My mother grew up during the depression, one of twelve children. Her family never had much meat, but they always had potatoes. I have often wondered how she continued to love potatoes after having so many as a child. She should have become sick of them.

So when I was a child, there were always plenty of potatoes at almost every meal. I now relish a little variety—rice and pastas, for example—but I still have to have my potatoes.

Potatoes have become a symbol of abundance to me, too.

I came so that they might have life and have it more abundantly. Jn 10:10

Growing Old in the Lord

She bends over to tend her flowers. They are but a shade of their former loveliness, when she had more energy to care for them. She smiles as I drive up with her two great-grandchildren, greets us at the car door, and ushers us in for lemonade. The bouquet in her hand is carefully placed in a waiting vase. Their fragrance mixes with the fresh June air and fills the corner of the room.

Grandpa joins us, putting down his paper and turning off the baseball game. Nothing is more important to him than his great-grandkids. He walks slowly into the kitchen to his store of hidden goodies. "Tookie, Gampa," my son says in confident expectation. It's part of the ritual. A visit to great-grandma and great-grandpa would be incomplete without it.

We talk about the weather, family, days gone by, days to come. For people in their eighties, my grandparents spend a lot of time keeping up on current affairs. Then as the sun begins to set, I pack my tired children into the car and promise to come back soon.

Grandpa gives them one more cookie, "for the road," and we drive away.

Planted in the house of the LORD, /they shall flourish in the courts of our God. /They shall bear fruit even in old age, always vigorous and sturdy. Ps 92:14-15

In My Temple

How good it is to be here, I tell myself. I have sneaked away. Away from TV, away from dirty dishes, away from screaming children. Away to be with you, my God. The sky is covered in a mantle of green. Bits of blue break through the leaf-covered branches. I am alone in my temple, away in the woods. I have come to worship, to praise, to be with my God in this place only God could have created.

The woods are still and yet stirring with activity as ants brush by and bees buzz and the morning sun rises to heat the day. I sit and am alone with you. Yet I am not alone, for multitudes come with me, inside me. I carry them with me to prayer and place them into your hands for your care.

Though it's but an hour, I am renewed and refreshed.

Better one day in your courts /than a thousand elsewhere. Ps 84:11

Indulgence

Outside, my children play, while inside I sit and balance the checkbook—trying to account for every penny. The ice cream truck rides by and my children run inside in anticipation.

I tell them no, and they walk out disappointed. It would be so easy if all I had to do was give in to their whims and see them happy, but I know that doesn't work. The more I give my children the more they want, the more they expect, the more they demand. They are no more happy (nor less unhappy), it seems, for my indulging them.

So as a mother I must draw the line between grace and over-indulgence. I must keep from squelching their young expectations while still imparting a sense of the practical realities of life.

But then I run outside and buy them their cones.

It is the Lord's blessing that brings wealth,
/and no effort can substitute for it. Prv 10:22

Butterfly

"Flybutter, Mama," her toddler exclaims and points.

"I see the flybutter," she tells her daughter. A beautiful monarch butterfly floats by on the wind. Only a short while ago it was encased in a cocoon. And before that it was an ugly caterpillar—no resemblance to this beauty.

She looks at this child of her older years, a butterfly who grew in the cocoon of her womb then burst forth, suddenly, with awe and wonder.

Therefore, we are not discouraged; rather, although our outer self is wasting away, our inner self is being renewed day by day. For this momentary light affliction is producing for us an eternal weight of glory beyond all compassion.
2 Cor 4:16-17

Birth

What's that I feel? Something's going on. There's this strange movement unlike any I've felt before. It's not like all the bouncing around I've felt this past month as you prepared for my coming. All of that cleaning and rearranging—I could tell you were anticipating something.

Now you seem excited and agitated, happy and yet worried at the same time. Something big is happening that will change both of our lives forever, won't it? I feel pressure, pushing. The warm fluid surrounding me is gone. I feel myself moving down a dark tunnel to a dull light. The light gets brighter.

I'm scared, Mother, until you hold me at your breast.

Jesus spoke to them again, saying, "I am the light of the world. Whoever follows me will not walk in darkness, but will have the light of life." Jn 8:12

Confidence

The horse's body is strong and muscular beneath my own. He's wild and free and powerful as we ride through forest glades and lush pastures. We are one, this beast and I.

My daughter joins us today. She's just learning. I show her how to canter, how to gallop, how to gently guide, how to show this animal who's boss.

"You mustn't be afraid," I tell her. "He'll sense your fear and take advantage of it. Approach your horse with confidence, even if you're unsure."

So, also, dear daughter, must you approach life. Keep your head high—be confident, stay in control. Approach life with self-confidence and be master of it!

Therefore, do not throw away your confidence;
it will have great recompense. You need
endurance to do the will of God and receive
what he has promised. Heb 10:35

The Bride

"Mommy, I have a boyfriend," my five year old stood in the hallway in her underwear and announced with great pleasure. Oh, no! Call the nearest convent! I've got to get her away from all those men waiting to lure her away from me.

"That's nice, honey, what's his name," I say instead. And so it all began. They start so young, don't they? Looking for that special someone who will take them away from you.

Twenty years have passed in but a moment since that day. My little girl is now a woman. There have been a lot of different boys, then men, since. Some have been better than the others, but none of them have been good enough for her, until this one.

"You'd better be good to her," I whisper to him as they leave the wedding reception.

She's still my five-year-old standing in the hallway.

———————————

As a young man marries a virgin, /your Builder
shall marry you; /And as a bridegroom rejoices
in his bride /so shall your God rejoice in you.
Is 62:5

Toads and Frogs

"Mommy, I'm never going to trust you again!"

I hear his shout reverberating out the open window even above the roar of the lawnmower. I shut the machine off and call to my young son.

"Come out here. What's the matter?"

"You said you were only going to do the front."

"I know, but look how bad it is back here."

"But you said you were only going to mow the front. I knew you'd end up doing all of it."

"But I didn't promise we'd do anything when I was done."

"I know, but I wanted to talk to you."

So we sit on the porch swing and we talk about matters of importance to an eight-year-old—toads and frogs, fishing, soccer, and summer vacation. After fifteen minutes he grabs his bat and ball and goes off in search of his friends. I'm free to return to the work that waited.

I called upon your name, O Lord, /from the bottom of the pit; /You heard me call, "Let not your ear /be deaf to my cry for help!" /You came to my aid when I called to you; /you said, "Have no fear!" Lam 3:55-57

Dead Skunk

"Yuck, smells like skunk," my son moans.

"Why do they smell like that when they are hit by a car?" my daughter asks.

"It's a defense, whenever they sense danger they let off that odor," I explain. "Even when they're dying."

God equipped us mothers with defense mechanisms, too. Whenever we feel our children are under attack, we start to fight back. It's mother-nature. Yet sometimes our defenses just aren't adequate for our surroundings. They don't always work.

We let off our last line of defense, like a skunk, helplessly, in vain, squirting odor at an approaching car.

For all about me are evils beyond count; /my sins so overcome me I cannot see. /They are more than the hairs of my head; /my courage fails me. /LORD, graciously rescue me! /Come quickly to help me, LORD! Ps 40:13-14

A Follower's Prayer

Don't ask this mother to chair such and such a committee. Don't make me fill a position where I am separated from the others, set apart and an easy target. Let me stay in the rank and file, where we can complain together about the lack of leadership!

———————————————

"Come after me, and I will make you fishers of men." Mk 1:17

Me

Today I celebrate a birthday. Maybe you can celebrate with me. What comes to mind is that ritual ceremony celebrated almost thirty years ago when I became a Girl Scout. I remember crossing over a bridge and looking into a mirror, representing a pond, and seeing my own reflection. How little I knew myself then.

I look in the mirror today and I see . . . not just a mother, not just a wife, not just a woman, not just a worker, not just a citizen, not just a friend, not just a writer, but myself. All these entities rolled into one and yet greater than their sum total. I see the person who is me.

Today I give myself the greatest gift of all—the whole me. The only me in the universe. Happy Birthday to me.

"The kingdom of heaven is like a net thrown into the sea, which collects fish of every kind. When it is full they haul it ashore and sit down to put what is good into buckets. What is bad they throw away. Thus it will be at the end of the age." Mt 13:47-48

> *Free*

I still believe that the best things in life are free. The best times I have with my kids are trips to the park or lake, or hikes in the woods with picnic lunches. There are no vendors here enticing my children with outrageously priced junk food or cheaply made, expensive souvenirs like you find at fairs and festivals. The fun is free, the company is good, and I don't have to wait for hours in long lines. I don't have to contend with crowds and distractions or fear losing my children. I don't have to worry about the day being spoiled because I won't buy that certain something they set their hearts on.

Of course my children don't necessarily agree with me. As they get older, trips to the park pale in comparison to trips to a mall or fair. And their negative attitude makes all the difference between an enjoyable day and a miserable day for us all.

So we compromise. We stay home. They get to play with their friends and I get to sit on my porch swing and watch the sunset.

At least it's free.

"I have neither silver nor gold, but what I do have I give you." Acts 3:6

Flies

I'm told Teresa of Avila compared the many distractions that can enter our prayer time to flies at a picnic. Let them come and go without too much notice, she advised. If you chase after them, you may miss the whole meal. And besides, once one leaves, another is sure to replace it.

My distractions are my children; housework waiting undone; conflicts at work that need to be resolved; letters unwritten; calls to be made; errands to run. Such are the flies that ruin my daily prayer.

So I follow Teresa's suggestion and turn all of these distractions over to God and concentrate on the meal. And somehow I am filled.

May (you) have strength to comprehend with all the holy ones what is the breadth and length and height and depth, and to know the love of Christ that surpasses knowledge, so that you may be filled with all the fullness of God. Eph 3:18-19

Toys

My children have come to expect every meal they eat out to come with a toy. The toy takes precedence over the meal itself. Their attention is diverted from the main event.

Our consumer society is always trying to divert us from the main event. The "things" we possess take precedence over our selves, our loved ones, our God.

Couples preparing for marriage, for example, are more concerned about the clothes, the flowers, the reception, than about the vows they are exchanging. At church, the behavior of our children, the songs we sing, the trappings in the sanctuary all take precedence over the main event—the breaking of the bread and the fellowship we share.

The toys become more important than the meal.

"Therefore I tell you, do not worry about your life, what you will eat, or about your body, what you will wear. Is not life more than food and the body more than clothing? Look at the birds in the sky; they do not sow or reap, they gather nothing into barns, yet your heavenly Father feeds them. Are not you more important than they?" Mt 6:25-26

The Meeting

I have a top level meeting to go to today. It's a meeting with myself. I need to negotiate a new contract with vacation time, sick leave, and built-in promotions.

The career-woman-in-me fights with me-as-mother over child care arrangements, the mother throwing guilt into the face of the aspiring professional seeking to establish herself. The housekeeper-in-me is appalled at the state of affairs on the homefront. The wife nags about bills, the mistress argues for more time with her husband for romantic evenings and weekend hideaways. The student wants more time to read and reflect and take classes. And the child-I-still-am wants more time to play. All these parts of me are fighting over one single limited body—mine. They all demand my limited resources. Somehow we all need to reach an agreement that all of us can live with.

The meeting is called to order.

"If a kingdom is divided against itself, that kingdom cannot stand. And if a house is divided against itself, that house will not be able to stand." Mk 3:24-25

Worry

Her children may be out of sight, but she's yet to get them out of her mind. She worries about how her daughter is raising the grandchildren. She worries about the escapades of her son at college.

Worrying is a full-time job for a mother. If she didn't worry, what would she do with her time?

Maybe she could go back to school, get a degree, start another career. Perhaps she could write a book, or take up painting. Maybe she could start that business she's always talked about. Or maybe her husband could retire early and they could take the trips they've always dreamed of. But no, she's already got a full-time job . . . as a worrier.

Her children need her to worry about them. After all, the things she worries about seldom happen. A mother's worry wards off the very things she worries about.

I want you to know how great a struggle I am having for you. Col 2:1

Fire and Rain

The rain pours down gently on the parched earth, drenching it, soothing it, like a salve on a wound. The children sleep late under its spell, and I let them. I think about my friend and her family.

The fire of her flame burned too bright till it devoured, consumed, burned all that it touched. Fire, when harnessed and used for light and heat, is a blessing. When it is out of control, however, it is destructive and needs healing water to put an end to its ravages. In an early burst of motherly zeal, she gave too much to her children—denying herself and her relationship with her spouse—all from a burning desire to be a good mother.

In the process she produced cinder and ashes where there was meant to be a family.

God, pour your gentle rain upon her and upon her family, so that they may all heal and grow closer to you through this purge by fire.

Let justice descend, O heavens, like dew from above, /like gentle rain let the skies drop it down. /Let the earth open and salvation bud forth; /let justice also spring up! /I, the Lord, have created this. Is 45:8

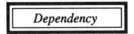

Dependency

There is some truth to the saying that if mothers want a job done right, they should do it themselves. The danger is, however, that we may get the job done the way we want it, but at the cost of keeping our families dependent on us.

So what if your husband doesn't prepare meals the way you do? At least he cooks. Who cares if your children don't fold the laundry the right way? They are building self-reliance and independence. Of course the babysitter doesn't care for your children the way you would. That's a small price to pay for letting you and your children know they can survive without you.

So let some things get done "wrong." It may be the "right" solution.

Jesus said to her, "Woman, how does your concern affect me? My hour has not yet come." His mother said to the servers, "Do whatever he tells you." Jn 2:4-5

Fireworks

Whistle, pop, snap, crackle, bang. Ooooohs and aaaahs as visions of color spread across the sky. We wait in anticipation of the next explosion.

My one daughter jumps and covers her ears, not sure whether to laugh or cry.

My other daughter likes the explosions, the noise and excitement, the unexpectedness of it all.

One child clings to me, the other stands enthralled.

So different children are. Like the many shapes and colors in the fireworks.

———————————

There are different kinds of spiritual gifts but the same Spirit; there are different forms of service but the same Lord; there are different workings but the same God who produces all of them in everyone. 1 Cor 12:4-6

The Will

Now that we have children, it's time to make out a will. Whatever for, I ask? We've nothing of value. The bank owns our house, the car company owns our one good car, and the other barely runs. If I die, my husband gets everything anyway.

But what if we both should die? Who will care for our children? What a distressing thought! Surely we won't die so young. Surely one of us will live to raise the children. To whom could we leave such a sacred trust? Whom do we know who would love our children as much as we do? Who would care for them as if they were their own?

I'd rather deny the whole thing, but it's impossible. If we don't choose someone, some court will determine what's best for our children. So we must decide, and now, if we are to be the responsible parents we want to be.

When Jesus saw his mother, and the disciple there whom he loved, he said to his mother, "Woman, behold your son." Then he said to the disciple, "Behold your mother." And from that hour the disciple took her into his home.
Jn 19:26-27

Gardeners

How does your garden grow? What you tend to is what grows. If you cultivate negative thoughts and anger, they will fester and get bigger. If you focus on your worries, they will blossom.

But if you leave your negative thoughts alone and concentrate on the positive, the negatives will dwindle for lack of care and the positives will bloom. You can always find reasons to be joyful. You can discover new opportunities to give thanks. You can nurture a more peaceful presence. If you water these flowers they will grow strong and turn towards the sun. You will have a beautiful garden rising high above the weeds and thorns.

Mothers are first and foremost gardeners.

Complete your outdoor tasks, /and arrange your work in the field; /afterward you can establish your house. Prv 24:27

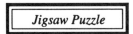

Jigsaw Puzzle

All of the little pieces of the jigsaw puzzle fit together somehow. If you work at it long enough, they all fit eventually. And you always have the big picture on the box to guide you.

The little pieces of my life don't fit together, however. I'm missing crucial parts here and there. Every now and then I come across a new piece and several other pieces fall into place. But then I reach another impasse and go for days, months, or years with no new insights.

And then there are those interlocking places where my life is entwined with others. It seems we form one massive jigsaw puzzle together, without end.

I'm trying to put all the pieces together, but sometimes it seems I have no box top to consult.

Then Moses went up from the plains of Moab to Mount Nebo, the headland of Pisgah which faces Jericho, and the LORD showed him all the land. Dt 34:1

Gossamer Web

Ah, those little ways in which we mothers manipulate. We trap our children like flies in a spider web. It's all unspoken and guarded. A gift here, a small thoughtfulness there. All subtle ways to control without having to admit our own natures.

We wish our children to be one way, so we cajole and model to get what we want. When we want them to be more appreciative of us, for example, we tell them how much we appreciate them and hope they'll say the same in return. When that doesn't happen, we add another resentment to our store to be brought out later in the heat of battle.

We pressure our children to do what we want and to be whom we want. We trap them in gossamer web to which they either remain stuck or from which they finally, angrily break free.

And we are left wondering how it happened.

———————————————

His confidence is but a gossamer thread /and his trust is a spider's web. /He shall rely upon his family, but it shall not last; /he shall cling to it, but it shall not endure. Jb 8:14-15

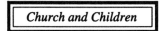

Church and Children

Church and children do not mix. I realize this too late as my youngsters squirm and talk all through the homily. They wiggle and dance up and down the pews during the most sacred of times. I'm wrung out like a dishrag from my constant battle to maintain a calm composure and ignore their antics in the vain hope they will stop if not encouraged by my attention.

Just when I'm ready to run out of church, tears stinging in embarassment, the priest holds up the cup and plate and my three-year-old shouts in a stage whisper for all to hear, "There's Jesus!"

Maybe church and children do mix.

_____

Out of the mouths of babes and infants /you
have drawn a defense against your foes.
Ps 8:3

Try

She reaches for just one drink. I can handle it, she thinks, but she knows it's a lie. One drink will lead to another.

"Mom, is something wrong?" her daughter asks, suddenly appearing from her bedroom.

"No, honey, I'm fine. Go back to bed."

The woman fumbles for the list of phone numbers. Names of people from the AA group she had attended.

"Hello," she says, "I need help."

If she can't do it for herself right now, at least she can try to do it for her children.

"When an unclean spirit goes out of a person it roams through arid regions searching for rest but finds none. Then it says, 'I will return to my home from which I came.' But upon returning, it finds it empty, swept clean, and put in order."
Mt 12:43-44

Precious Memories

"Back when I was a child . . ." he'd begin. The warning signal went off in my young brain. Here we go again, I'd think, another dumb story to show me how good I have things. My dad's reminiscences about his childhood were always tedious reminders to be grateful.

Now I do the same thing to my own kids. I remind them of how thankful they should be for all the blessings they have. I try to instill gratitude this way, but it doesn't work. They can't know how good they have things. They have so little experience with which to compare their lives. They will acquire that only over time.

Maybe someday they'll look back on my stories with the same feelings I have for Dad's. His are no longer boring to me, but precious memories of my blessed childhood.

Precious is his memory, like honey to the taste,
/like music at a banquet. Sir 49:1

Tears, Part 2

Why do tears have such a bad reputation among mothers? Why do we so often consider them a sign of our weakness? Tears are natural stress releasers. They are cleansers, flushing the body and soul of pent-up frustrations and hurts. They can be far more helpful than running a mile or smashing a punching bag. Sometimes hurt masquerades as anger, when what we really need is a good cry.

Some days, the only way I make it through is by allowing myself ten minutes to cry. The stresses of a mother's life are many. We can keep on forging ahead, denying the pain that is there; or we can stop to cry, and then forge ahead.

Just give me ten minutes alone to cry, and then I'll be all right.

And Jesus wept. Jn 11:35

Running on Empty

When the gas gauge in your car reads "E," you know its time for a fill up. To neglect that sign could result in being stranded somewhere without any means of getting home. When your stomach starts growling you know it's time for a meal. To disregard your body for too long may result in illness or a hospital stay. When you know your spirit needs renewal, to put it off could be disastrous to your eternal salvation.

Why do we mothers have such a hard time recognizing our own spiritual needs? We worry about everyone else's prayer life, but we think that we can somehow get along without one of our own.

We're running on empty.

The report about him spread all the more, and great crowds assembled to listen to him and to be cured of their ailments, but he would withdraw to deserted places to pray.
Lk 5:15-16

The Prince

Mommy, I'm only two years old. I don't know how to tell you how I feel, but feel I do. My few words are so inadequate for all I long to tell you.

You are my whole world. I worship you. I fear you. You hold all the power in this little world of mine, yet I manipulate you with the slightest wriggle of my little finger. I'm at your mercy for my many wishes, my desires, my needs, but please don't give in to me all the time.

I don't really know what's best for me even though I rule here like a little prince.

Mom, save me from myself.

"Oh Lord, my God, you have made me your servant, king to succeed my father David; but I am a mere youth, not knowing at all how to act." 1 Kg 3:7

A Mother's Child

My pager goes off. It's my turn to go out on call with the volunteer ambulance team.

We rush to the scene, sirens blaring, turning them off as we approach the address. No need to cause unnecessary alarm. My partner and I jump out and enter the home. An eighty-two-year-old woman waits. We check her vitals, give her oxygen, ask all the necessary questions of her spouse, transport her by cot to the ambulance and start for the hospital. The spouse rides in front while I ride in back with the woman. My partner keeps the sirens off. The old lady is breathing comfortably now.

I hold the woman's hand throughout the ride and offer reassurance. After all, she may be someone's mother; and she most certainly is some mother's child.

Listen to your father who begot you, /and despise not your mother when she is old. Prv 23:22

Simplify

Simplify, simplify, simplify, I tell myself. Yet each time I try, something new seems to creep in to complicate life.

Having children both complicated my life immeasurably and forced me to simplify it. The simplest task—like running to the store for a bottle of milk—became a major undertaking when a couple of pre-schoolers were in tow.

Put on their coats and hats. Buckle them into their car seats. Take them out of their car seats. Hold hands as we cross the street. "Don't touch," repeated time and time again, up and down the aisles. Vice grips on their shoulders lest they slip away and get lost. "No, No, No," to candy. The inevitable tantrums at the check-out lane. All for a bottle of milk.

So I simplify. We go without milk until Dad gets home!

"Take nothing for the journey, neither walking stick, nor sack, nor food, nor money, and let no one take a second tunic. Whatever house you enter, stay there and leave from there."
Lk 9:3-4

Witch Babysitters

I've got a great idea for making money. I call it the Witch Babysitting Service, and I would be one of its best customers. No more nice babysitters who give my children snacks and allow them to watch endless TV! The next time I come home to an uptight, strung-out babysitter and my children bouncing off the wall hours past their bedtime, I'd just call the Witch Babysitting Service.

I'd ask them to send over one of their oldest crones with bags full of knitting needles, eyes of newts, and pickled toads. As she sat and knitted, she'd reach in and munch a toad or two—being sure to offer one to the children. The child who made a single peep would promptly be turned into a mouse and chased by the family cat. The children would suddenly develop an overpowering urge to go to bed. Just to make sure they weren't fooling around upstairs, the witch sitter would hop on her trusty broom and peer in their bedroom windows.

Just the threat of witch babysitters would put terror into the fiercest child's heart. After one visit, children would be models of good behavior for all future babysitters. I'll make millions.

Then Saul said to his servants, "Find me a woman who is a medium, to whom I can go to seek counsel through her." His servants answered him, "There is a woman in Endor who is a medium." 1 Sam 28:7

Summer Romance

My fifteen-year-old daughter is "in love." It brings back bittersweet memories of my own first love—excitement, longing, confusion and despair, all rolled into one. What a sweet, innocent summer that was. Certain "oldies" still bring back those memories, and I wonder where that boy is, how he's doing, if he's married with children. But I don't really want to know the answers. I want him to be eternally young in my memory. I hope I'm that way for him, too—always young, always fifteen, and always in love.

I want my daughter to have that same experience, but now isn't such an innocent age. Fifteen-year-olds in love sometimes hop into bed together. That produces so many more powerful feelings than I had. So many hurts await her if she gives in to those passions. The innocence of young love can dissolve into unwanted pregnancies and even AIDS.

How can I make her understand? Dear child, the world is too terrible and too wonderful for you to fully comprehend. Please be innocent a while longer.

Strengthen me with raisin cakes, /refresh me with apples, /for I am faint with love. Song 2:5

Friends and Mothers

"Brrr," she shivers and runs through the sprinkler. The water from the hose feels like ice on her skin. Even in the hot sun it's hard to take such extreme cold. She stays on the edge of the sprinkler's reach, wetting her feet and little else.

"Come on, run through the middle," I tell her. "Get wet or I'll turn it off." But she's content to stay on the fringes, not daring to run boldly through the middle. She's quiet and content and laughing, and so am I.

One little step at a time, my daughter ventures forth. Tentatively, she approaches this big world.

I resist the urge to pick her up and run through the sprinkler with her. She's got to do it on her own. I go inside for a short while. When I come back she has been joined by her friend from next door. Hand in hand they run through the center of the sprinkler.

After all, that's what friends—not mothers—are for.

He who is a friend is always a friend, /and a brother is born for the time of stress.
Prv 17:17

Martha and Mary

I find it hard to believe that Luke had any idea how the simple story of Jesus visiting two sisters would be interpreted after him. How Martha would get the short end of the stick, for generations epitomizing the complaining shrew, unable to sit for a moment's rest. Mary doesn't fare that much better, for she is the shirker of her fair share of the work and part of the reason Martha is so dour and joyless.

Isn't there a little bit of Martha and Mary in all mothers? Rather than two extremes, I'd rather think that Martha and Mary were both vibrant, alive women, both full of life but maybe approaching it from differ-ent perspectives. Mary wasn't necessarily that different from her sister Martha, except that she somehow recognized how important it was to listen to Jesus. If this meant other good deeds, even the good deed of offering hospitality, needed to be put aside for a while, then so be it.

Sometimes being true to the kingdom means going against the mainstream—to sit at the feet of the teacher when the rest of the women are busy in the kitchen.

Martha, burdened with much serving, came to him and said, "Lord, do you not care that my sister has left me by myself to do the serving? Tell her to help me." Lk 10:40

Scraped Knees and Other Booboos

"Mo-o-om!" the wail was heard all over the neighborhood. Another fallen child: from a tree limb, over a curb, off a bike. Scrapes and scratches, cuts and bruises—the many little mishaps of childhood. All the moms on the block stick their heads out doors or windows, ears attuned to the unique howls of their own children.

Scrapes are washed, cuts are bandaged, and booboos kissed. All part of a normal day in the neighborhood. Children are hugged and kissed and patted and sent on their way, back out into the world to play.

If only all of life's problems could be solved so easily.

If a brother or sister has nothing to wear and has no food for the day, and one of you says to them, "Go in peace, keep warm, and eat well," but you do not give them the necessities of the body, what good is it? Jas 2:15-16

Balloons

I'm hooked. I'm addicted. Not to drugs or gambling or shopping, but to the chase. Chasing after the trucks carrying hot air balloons to their launch point.

There's something about those big balloons. They hang so still in the air, floating lightly. They are powered solely by the wind. All they can do is rise and fall to catch the breeze, much like a sailboat does in water. They are unpredictable and difficult to steer.

They are like kids, and I'm addicted to kids, too.

"The wind blows where it wills, and you can hear the sound it makes, but you do not know where it comes from or where it goes; so it is with everyone who is born of the Spirit."
Jn 3:8

Sand Castles

The sky above shines azure blue, meeting the green of the line of trees and the bluegreen of the lake. My children run to the sand and bury their feet in the warm gold before testing the water.

I sit back and watch. I hear their screams of delight as they splash and kick and run to and fro—one minute appearing at my side, the next back in the water. Happily they play. They build sand castles and discover shells and capture frogs as the warm breeze blows the pages of my book. I am distracted by the beauty of creation, unable to focus on my reading.

I remove my sandals and bury my feet deep into the warm sand. Then I burst forth and run to build sand castles with my children.

How lovely your dwelling, /O Lord of hosts!
Ps 84:2

Anticipation

My children are driving me crazy. Like a fool I informed them last night that I would take them to the fair this afternoon. The morning has been spent in anticipation of the event. Rather than go about their normal daily activities, they keep asking me if it's time for lunch yet. They sit and pick at each other and already are fighting over who will sit in the front seat of the car.

God is much smarter than I am. God doesn't give us much notice of what is going to happen. We would all act like my children, sitting around in anticipation of the event. Or, like some in the early Christian community awaiting the second coming, we'd not do any work.

Better that we don't know what God has in store for us, the good or the painful. God will let us know what we need to know, when we need to know it.

The people were filled with expectation.
Lk 3:15

Phone Call

The phone rings and brings terrible news into my peaceful existence. The phone rings and what was an ordinary day turns into a nightmare.

Dad's in the hospital with a heart attack. They don't think he'll make it. Can I come soon? Of course I'll come. Immediately, I say.

I make hurried arrangements for the kids to stay at a friend's after school. I let my husband know where to pick them up. I'll come home, he says. We'll drive together. I can't hear him through the roar in my head. I can't think straight, can't see straight. My mother needs me. I must go now. That's all I can think.

Mom needs me.

Fear not, for I am with you; /from the east I will bring back your descendants, /from the west I will gather you. /I will say to the north; Give them up! /and to the south; Hold not back! /Bring back my sons from afar, /and my daughters from the ends of the earth. Is 43:5-6

Mosquitoes

There's a mosquito in my son's bedroom, keeping him awake. This means I'm awake too. I go into his room, turn on the light, and together we try to find the elusive creature.

"Are you sure?" I ask.

"It was in here. I heard it buzzing. It's keeping me awake."

"Well, maybe it's gone now. Try to go back to sleep. If it comes back cover your head with your sheet."

I turn off the light and groggily head for my own bed, only to be awakened minutes later.

"Mom, it's back. I can't sleep." Neither can I.

I never could understand why God created mosquitoes. A more worthless creature I've never known. All it does is suck blood and spread disease. A constant irritant. I take great pleasure in smacking them whenever I can.

The various winged insects that walk on all fours are loathsome to you. Lv 11:20

What's Important

My son has a great knack for seeing what's really important and what's not. What is really important— the clothes we wear or the friends we play with? Messes to clean up or science projects to experiment with? Tied shoes or climbed trees? Teeth brushed or cartoons watched? Even eating supper pales in comparison to the pleasures of playing with the boys next door.

It's a constant struggle to get my son to see the importance of routine chores. After all, what's so important about hanging up your coat or taking care of your backpack? It's much more urgent to find out what's for snack. Time is much too precious to waste on non-essentials.

He recently discovered that if he wears his clothes to bed it saves getting dressed in the morning.

Who can argue with such logic?

---

*Why is one day more important than another,
/when it is the sun that lights up every day?
Sir 33:7*

$$\boxed{\textit{Help}}$$

The newspaper today reported that a mother tried to kill herself and her two children. "I thought it would be better if we all went together," she said. Better for whom: for her, for her children, for society?

What kind of world does this mother live in if this is her only way out of her problems?

How do we reach such mothers to let them know there are other solutions? How do we let them know there are people who would help?

And where are those people?

LORD, my God, I call out by day; /at night I cry aloud in your presence. /Let my prayer come before you; /incline your ear to my cry. /For my soul is filled with troubles; /my life draws near to Sheol. Ps 88:2-4

Both Ways

Barn swallows go swooping across the sky, and I long to fly with them. They make dramatic turns and loops like a daredevil pilot and then pull up out of a deep plunge, just missing the ground.

I long to swoop in such utter abandon. But for now my feet are rooted to the ground by responsibilities. Children to care for, clothing to mend, jobs to be done. They tie me down and fetter my soul.

Then I look at the oak tree in our yard. How beautiful it stands, limbs reaching high into the blue sky yet trunk planted firmly into the ground, rooted deep in the soil. Suddenly I realize, I can have both.

I, too, can reach into the sky, even though my feet remain stuck in the ground. I, too, can dig roots deeply into this earth, yet still soar in the air.

In fact, the deeper my roots, the higher I can reach.

Long life is in her right hand, /in her left are riches and honor; /Her ways are pleasant ways, /and all her paths are peace; /She is a tree of life to all who grasp her, /and he is happy who holds her fast. Prv 3:16-18

$$\boxed{\textit{Authority}}$$

Why is it that we women are so quick to give away our authority to a man—any man who may come along regardless of his ability? And why are men so quick to try to take this authority? Why is it that we women are so slow to listen to ourselves and each other? Why do we find affirmation from men so important in our lives?

Is it that women have been conditioned to give up power and authority in order to have the relationships that we so desire, or that men have been trained to ignore relationships in order to have power?

We'd all better figure it out. For the sake of our children, if not for our own.

————————————————

Woman is not independent of man or man of woman in the Lord. For just as woman came from man, so man is born of woman; but all things are from God. 1 Cor 11:11-12

Lemonade Stand

My son has hatched another get-rich-quick scheme. Like most of his plans, it involves me. I am to be the financial backer, paying for all of his initial overhead. I mix the lemonade while he makes the sign, "Lemonade: 10 cents a glass."

My son needs to learn about money. Too often his plans to save for something vanish into candy bars and ice cream as his allowance burns a hole in his pocket. Now he's seen other kids making money through garage sales or selling treats, and he feels it's time for him to get in on this easy cash.

I encourage him in these efforts. It's well worth my contribution to keep him occupied and—besides—I may one day be the mother of the multi-millionaire owner of the newest chain of fast food eateries!

Be diligent in these matters, be absorbed in them, so that your progress may be evident to everyone. 1 Tm 4:15

Hoops

How bad do you want it? They say jump, I say how high. I guess that's how bad I want it.

At this rate I should be a circus acrobat, flying through flaming hoops.

The Flaming Madonna.

"What the eyes see is better than what the desires wander after." This also is vanity and a chase after wind. Eccl 6:9

Roses without Thorns

She reaches for the bright red flower before I can grab her and her finger is pricked by a thorn. A look of complete dismay and betrayal enters her cherubic two-year-old face. She can't quite believe that anything so beautiful would hurt her. She grabbed too quickly, without caution, as only a small child does. She believes she is queen of all her domain. Yet there are thorns lurking amid her roses.

If only I could give my children roses without thorns. I long so to allow them to experience all the beauty and pleasure of life without the ugliness and pain. Instead, I must teach them to approach life with some caution, rather than with their natural, wild-eyed abandon. I have to teach them that even the most temptingly beautiful objects—and people—may have thorns hidden within them.

For whatever reason, God surrounded roses with thorns. That doesn't mean we can't enjoy them.

We just have to approach them carefully.

Discretion will watch over you, /understanding will guard you. Prv 2:11

General Mom

It all began when the first child arrived. No one was a more dedicated mother. She hardly left her baby's side. She carried him close to her heart in a little pouch while she did her housework. He slept in a small bassinet close to her bed. She breast fed him upon demand.

Then child number two came along. Her shoulders began to droop. She didn't as readily offer the teat to this whinesome baby. She was not quite as patient with her two-year-old's tantrums. She began to feel pulled in many directions by her children and her own inner needs that were being denied.

Almost overnight, it seemed, she changed. The tender young mother lovingly dangling baby at breast began to snap and push her young offspring out of the nest. She began to counter their demands with her own. No longer the selfless mother, she became a drill sergeant marching her little charges to her regime. And then was born . . .

General Mom.

Enlighten them in regard to the decisions and regulations, showing them how they are to live and what they are to do. Ex 18:20

The Complete Me

I've always been ambitious. I've just never allowed myself to admit it. It was too unwomanly. I've also always been competitive, in my own way, within certain parameters. But I never wanted to appear too competitive, because that wasn't "right" for a gentlewoman. I'm also aggressive, but I only allow my aggressive nature to come out during card games and other games.

Aggression, ambition, competition have always been a part of me. I've just denied them for too long. Maybe they are the "masculine" part of me, but they make me more human, more complete.

I need to make sure my daughters—and my sons—understand that.

Compete well for the faith. Lay hold of eternal life, to which you were called when you made the noble confession in the presence of so many witnesses. 1 Tm 6:12

August 5

Mowing Lawns

Round and round I go, pushing our noisy lawnmower. I shut off the machine for a moment, only to have the noise keep on reverberating in my ears for several minutes. Then I begin again the never-ending job. Sometimes the cut grass blows in my face. I sneeze, pause momentarily, then begin again. Got to keep going. It seems I hardly finish before it's time to start again.

Sometimes my life also seems to go around and around in a never-ending circle. I hardly finish with one job, one chore, one activity before it's time to begin again. I never seem to be making any progress. And if I take a break and rest for too long, the "grass" is just longer and harder to cut when I do get around to it. Sometimes irritations fly up and hit me in the face, but I just sneeze them out and keep going. Often, the noise of my day reverberates in my ears even after I have shut down for the night.

Around and around I go, seemingly without end. For every step forward, I slide back ten. The only thing that's sure is that as I get older the pushing gets harder.

Is not man's life on earth a drudgery? /Are not his days those of a hireling? /He is a slave who longs for the shade, /a hireling who waits for his wages. /So I have been assigned months of misery, /and troubled nights have been told of for me. Jb 7:1-3

Life in the Here and Now

There's a whole other dimension of life out there that I've never experienced. It's called the world of the present.

I've lived most my life looking toward the future. First it was getting into grade school, then graduating from high school, then college. Then I eagerly awaited marriage, then that first child, then for the last child to get into school so I could pursue some other dreams of my own. Always that looking ahead, always that goal to strive for. No sooner was one accomplished than I grabbed another.

I never learned how to live in the present, but I'd better learn fast. Before I know it, all my futures will be my pasts.

Today is the future I longed for as a child. Someday it will be the past that I cherish. How can I learn to live life in the here and now?

"Seek first the kingdom [of God] and his righteousness, and all these things will be given you besides. Do not worry about tomorrow; tomorrow will take care of itself. Sufficient for a day is its own evil." Mt 6:33-34

A Mother's Prayer

She is dying, but all she can think about is who will care for her children.

She knows her husband can't do it alone. She wants him to find a new wife—a new woman to sleep in her bed, mother her children.

She prays only that she will make it through one more Christmas. One more Christmas with her precious little ones around her. Then she will die in peace.

Meanwhile, all she can think about is who will care for her children.

"When I was with them I protected them in your name that you gave me, and I guarded them, and none of them was lost." Jn 17:12

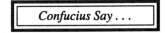

Confucius Say . . .

Confucius say there is no God.

Confucius never a mother.

Mothers know there is a reality that is more than we can see or even comprehend. We believe it because we've caught glimpses of it while watching our children play or sitting at their sickbeds or nursing them as babies. Only glimpses of the divine, but enough to believe. We have experienced a reality greater than ourselves, a power that is good and active in a world that at times seems given over to evil.

Confucius say there is no God. But Confucius' mother know better.

As he looked on, he was surprised to see that the bush, though on fire, was not consumed. So Moses decided, "I must go over to look at this remarkable sight, and see why the bush is not burned." Ex 3:3

Quality Time vs. Quantity Time

We mothers—especially if we are working outside the home—hear a lot about the need for "quality time" with our children. There seems to be an implication that, as long as we spend a certain amount of quality time with our children each day, we have fulfilled our maternal obligation. *Not so!* Our children need "quantity time"—lots of it—from their moms.

Of course, the opposite extreme is also true. It is possible for mothers to be physically around their children but never really "be there" for them. Mothers may be home with their kids but not present to them because their minds are elsewhere.

Children need both quality time and quantity time from us. Neither is sufficient alone. Each compliments the other. Our children need to learn both skills—how to be involved with and attentive to another, and how to simply spend time together, respecting each other's space but not necessarily relating.

In other words, they need a small quantity of quality time and a low quality of quantity time from us.

A time to seek, and a time to lose; /a time to keep, and a time to cast away. Eccl 3:6

Birthday Party

I survived yet another birthday party today. Ten eight-year-old boys tearing up my home.

Every year I have to compete with the last year. Each party has to be bigger and better. There's the competition with the other kids' mothers, who come up with creative new themes each year, spend months making homemade party favors and decorations, and hire a clown or some other live entertainer. The only entertainment my kids get is me turning different shades of red and purple from screaming. Who can compete with having your birthday party at some popular pizza or burger place? I give up.

Next year, no party. I don't care what the child psychiatrists say. There's got to be a better way. My son now has nine new toys to cram into his already overcrowded toy closet and is bouncing off the wall on a sugar high. Who says the only way to help our kids feel loved and special on their birthdays is through expending tons of energy and money babysitting someone else's kids? What's wrong with a quiet dinner at home with Mom and family?

I have a whole year to convince my son of this.

Then they sat down to eat and drink, and rose up to revel. Ex 32:6

"Make Me"

The thief on the cross challenged Jesus to prove he was God by saving himself and them. Jesus had the power to do this, yet he didn't—choosing instead to allow the natural course of life to unfold.

My kids challenge me all the time to do something that I can but won't. "Make me," they taunt. By sheer physical force I could "make them"—but I won't, and don't.

Just because it can be done, doesn't mean we should do it.

Let no one have contempt for your youth, but set an example for those who believe, in speech, conduct, love, faith, and purity.   1 Tm 4:12

The Experts

Knock, knock.

Can Patty come out to play?

Gosh, I wish I could, but there are dishes to wash, laundry to fold, meals to prepare, classes to attend, bills to pay, papers to write, presentations to prepare, worries to worry. Who can play in the face of so much responsibility?

Even the family puzzle I purchased recently is pursued with so much intensity on my part that it has lost any sense of fun. While watching cartoons with my kids, my mind wanders to work left undone.

Yet inside of me is a frustrated little girl who hasn't forgotten about tea parties and baby dolls and playing house, even though she's now busy with the real thing. It's been so long since I really played that I fear I don't know how to begin again.

I know: I'll ask my children. They're the experts at this.

Knock, knock.

The city shall be filled with boys and girls playing in her streets. Zec 8:5

Sharing Berries

"One for the bucket, two for me," my daughter says as she drops a deep blue berry into her bucket and pops two into her mouth. She doesn't contribute a lot to the number of berries we actually bring home, but she's content.

Come to think of it, her ratio really isn't that bad. Two-thirds for her, one third for the family bucket. That's even better than the biblical one out of ten. We should all be so generous with the fruits of our labor! If we were, there would be no want in this world. But we're not. We grudgingly dole out what little we contribute to the common good.

Of course, my daughter also benefits from the joint collection. She gets her share of the pies and jam I make from the berries. So it is for all who share. We all benefit from what we give to others. It all comes back in some way.

Cast your bread upon the waters; /after a long time you may find it again. Eccl 11:1

Pimples

My son and daughter spend hours in front of the mirror bemoaning their adolescent acne. They poke at their pimples, squeezing them, picking at them, covering them, creaming them. They do everything but leave them alone.

I tell them the story of the beautiful young woman who somehow had the ability to refrain from squeezing. She tolerated all those pussy bumps on her face. Her friends turned away in agony upon seeing her, fighting their own desire to reach out and squeeze. She allowed her pimples to pop naturally. She was confidant enough in her self-worth not to be bothered by what others might think or say. In the end, she was rewarded with a glowing complexion and no pock marks. (Of course, I never actually knew anyone like this woman, but the story was told to me when I was a teen and so I pass it on . . . to no avail.)

Wait a minute. What's that in the mirror. Augh, a pimple. I'm not supposed to have pimples! I'm a grown woman with teenagers. They are supposed to have the pimples, not me. Get out the face cream, hide it under make-up, lock the bathroom door so I can squeeze in privacy.

"Why do you notice the splinter in your brother's eye, but do not perceive the wooden beam in your own eye?" Mt 7:3

Habits

"Aw, Mom, I combed it yesterday," he moans.

"Well, do it again," I tell him. My son has a problem recognizing that some activities need to be done again and again, regardless of how many times he may have done them before. Why should he have to comb his hair every day? Or brush his teeth after every meal? Or go to the dentist every six months? Or make his bed every day?

I try to communicate that some activities give order to our world. They are the habits we do instinctively, without thinking. If we had to decide whether or not to do them each day, we would get nowhere fast. We'd be forced to think about every little task, rather than leaving our brain power for more important things.

Yes, son, you did it yesterday. And you will do it today, and tomorrow, until it becomes your second nature. Save your creativity and energy for life's real challenges.

"Since we desire that this people too should be undisturbed, our decision is that their temple be restored to them and that they live in keeping with the customs of their ancestors. Accordingly, please send them messengers to give them our assurances of friendship, so that, when they learn of our decision, they may have nothing to worry about but may contentedly go about their own business." 2 Mc 11:25-26

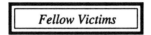

Fellow Victims

Her baby is a child of violence. The result of a horrible, violent attack. She could have had an abortion, but she didn't. So she lived with the terror of that night growing daily inside her—a constant reminder of what had been done to her.

Yet she knows her baby is as much an innocent victim as she was. There is a special bond between them, beyond even that of mother and child. She will give her baby up for adoption, but, still, there will be this bond.

The bond of fellow victims. And the incredible bond of motherly love that overcomes all evil.

No one has greater love than this, to lay down one's life for one's friends. Jn 15:13

Chamber of Horrors

Oh, if only I could be transported to the twenty-fifth century—just for my yearly check-ups. Going into today's medical offices for simple tests is like going into a chamber of horrors. Just the sight of some of the equipment they have for examining female organs is enough to send shivers of terror down my spine. We women are poked, probed and scraped, and long instruments are inserted into our vaginas—all in the name of good health! I can't help thinking how some of these same procedures are used in some countries to torture female prisoners. I also recall cases where similar objects are forcibly inserted into little girls' privates to abuse them.

But then I think of the days before anesthesia and x-rays and sterile instruments, and I appreciate our modern medical advances. Woman of the fifteenth century would surely envy us. Still, I dream of the day when medicine will be so advanced that a simple little box run over a fully clothed body will tell the doctors everything they need to know about a woman's condition.

Simon's mother-in-law was afflicted with a severe fever, and they interceded with him about her. He stood over her, rebuked the fever, and it left her. She got up immediately and waited on them. Lk 4:38-39

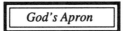

God's Apron

I've heard of one mother who would periodically throw her apron over her head in order to have some peace amidst the chaos of raucus children. Her children knew to not bother her when she was under her apron. That was her safe space.

I don't know whether this is a true story or not, but I can see a harried mother reaching her breaking point and throwing her apron over her head in desperation.

All mothers wear God's apron, whether we realize it or not.

We can throw it over our heads anytime we need to.

———————————

"Here," continued the LORD, "is a place near me where you shall station yourself on the rock. When my glory passes I will set you in the hollow of the rock and will cover you with my hand until I have passed by." Ex 33:21-22

Then and Now

"Out of my house," I'd scream and chase my youngsters out into the fresh air for their own good . . . and mine, too.

"Out, out, out," I'd yell. "Look at this mess you made!" Spills for me to wipe up. Toys for me to pick up. Clothes dropped on the floor right where they were taken off.

Seems like only yesterday I was yelling at them, kicking them out of the house, picking up after them, stumbling over their debris. Now my house is spotless. Oh, how I wish they were here again to run in and out, letting in the flies, tracking in the mud.

What I wouldn't give for a little less peace and quiet, a little more noise and clutter. Why can't those hectic days be rationed and saved for lonely days in the future? Why can't I trade some of the peacefulness of my life now for some of the chaos of twenty years ago?

Then I needed quiet.

Now I need noise.

Try to join me soon, for Demas, enamored of the present world, deserted me and went to Thessalonica, Crescens to Galatia, and Titus to Dalmatia. 2 Tm 4:9-10

> *Don't Just Do Something, Stand There*

We mothers place a high value on activity, any activity. Just so we keep on moving. Little value is seen in the ability to stand by and do nothing.

Now, I don't applaud laziness. If they gave grades for this vice, my children would all excel. They have thoroughly accomplished the skill of lying around while Mom runs circles around them.

But I do applaud the person who has the ability to stand back and wait, who takes time to assess a situation before plunging in and acting.

Maybe if mothers did this more often, our children would learn the difference between frantic activity and planned action.

This is the resting place, /give rest to the weary; /Here is repose— /but they would not listen. Is 28:12

Potty Mouths

"abcdefghijklmno qrstuvwxyz. You forgot to p!"

My children always laugh hilariously at this joke. There's nothing quite like pre-schooler humor. The best jokes all center on bodily functions. Anything that has to do with the "potty" will put children into hysterics. Where does their fascination with bodily functions come from, and whence the humor? And are we adults so different?

The most popular jokes for adults often still center on bodily functions, this time the sexual ones. We love to laugh hilariously at sexual references and double entendres. We have a huge vocabulary of words to describe sexual organs and sexual intercourse.

For those of declining years, once again many favorite jokes revolve around the aging and failure of certain body parts and functions.

Let's face it, adults continue to be as fixated on the human body as any two-year-old. Our knowledge becomes more mature and complex, maybe, but the fascination remains.

No foul language should come out of your mouths, but only such as is good for needed edification, that it may impart grace to those who hear. Eph 4:29

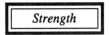

Strength

How to tell my kids that our dog has to be put to sleep? What words can I say to take away some of the pain; to ensure that this doesn't hurt any more than it has to? Give me some magic formula, God.

I know I have to be strong for my children's sake, but I don't feel so strong.

Who will be strong for me?

Answer when I call, my saving God. /In my troubles, you cleared a way; /show me favor; hear my prayer. Ps 4:2

Plucking Weeds

This summer, after a week's absence, I found my garden even more overrun with weeds than normally. I proceeded to pull them out, only to discover that I had pulled some of the plants with them.

The passage from Matthew's gospel about the weeds growing amongst the wheat came to mind. "If you pull up the weeds you might uproot the wheat along with them." As always, Jesus knew what he was talking about. We are all so intertwined and interconnected that we can't just pull out the bad without risking the good. The loss of any individual affects us all in ways we cannot fathom.

It's easy to be outraged over the needless killing of babies and children, but not so easy to feel the same outrage over the killing of a convicted murderer. I, too, like the rest of society, am disgusted with some of our convicted felons. It seems that hanging is too good for them. We have to pluck out these weeds, obviously, before they can choke any more of our plants. And then I remember Matthew 13:29, and I pause.

"The kingdom of heaven may be likened to a man who sowed good seed in his field. While everyone was asleep his enemy came and sowed weeds all through the wheat, and then went off. When the crop grew and bore fruit, the weeds appeared as well." Mt 13:24-26

Daddy's Girl

"You were the best present I ever got," Daddy used to say. "A baby girl for my birthday."

Even though I'm far from home and have children of my own, I'm still Daddy's girl.

Even when I'm old and gray, I'll still be Daddy's girl.

And even when my father is gone to be with his heavenly Father, I'll still be Daddy's girl.

I wouldn't want it any other way.

———————————

Our Father in heaven, /hallowed be your name.
Mt 6:9

Reprieve

I luxuriate in bed, listening for the first time in oh so long to the birds and other sounds of nature.

I sip my coffee and read the morning paper at my leisure, sitting on the porch swing. I bask in the morning sun, enjoying every ounce of this special day. My husband and I conduct a lovely conversation over a late breakfast.

We have been given a reprieve from child-rearing. The kids are at Grandma's.

This is the day the LORD has made, /let us rejoice in it and be glad. Ps 118:24

Visits with Grandchildren

The fast food restaurant is filled with grandparents and grandchildren. I watch as the children run here and there while the grandparents buy the food and carry it to tables. The weary elders sit down with a sigh as their active grandchildren head for the play area.

"I know why you have children when you're young," one grandmother comments. "I may have all this experience raising kids, but I have no energy. They are wearing me out."

I smile understandingly.

"Yes," another grandmother comments. "It's nice when they come to visit, but also nice when they go."

I sit and remember my own grandchildren's last visit. Some things are better when remembered.

———————————

Grandchildren are the crown of old men, /and the glory of children is their parentage.
Prv 17:6

Fireflies

My children delight in catching fireflies on warm August nights. The fireflies spark the night like so many blinking Christmas lights. Off and on. On and off. Just when you think you're going to catch one, off goes the light and it gets away.

In the same way our lives blink on and off: moments of joy, moments of sorrow; moments of light when we see everything clearly, and moments of darkness when we can't see a thing.

All moments come and go. The minute you think you've caught one, it's gone.

Then God said, "Let there be light," and there was light. Gn 1:3

Yesterday's Privilege

Isn't this how it works? What was a privilege yesterday becomes a right today and an obligation tomorrow. The special treat I gave my children yesterday they take as their right today. Before I know it, I'm under an obligation to keep providing it. One trip to the bakery for donuts on my day off becomes the norm and expectation for all my days off, robbing the treat of its specialness—at least in my eyes.

The same thing happens in all walks of life and with all age ranges. If for some reason yesterday's privilege has to be discontinued, we organize protests and bring lawsuits against companies, governments, schools, anyone we can think of.

We are fortunate that God doesn't treat us the way we treat each other.

If, therefore, you have courts for every day matters, do you seat as judges people of no standing in the church? I say this to shame you. Can it be that there is not one among you wise enough to settle a case between brothers?
1 Cor 6:4-5

The Other Man

He is usually younger than our husbands, or more handsome. How does that compare to our years together, the history we share? He can't give us that.

Don't throw away those years. Only a fool would do that.

Beloved fool, come to your senses before its too late, before your spouse, too, chasing after *his* own illusions, finds someone else.

Beloved fool, your husband doesn't want illusions. He just wants you.

Wisdom builds her house, /but Folly tears hers down with her own hands. Prv 14:1

Kid Time

Time is an extravagant commodity for children. Days seem years, minutes are hours. Time hangs on their hands in endless abundance.

My kids' sense of time is bound to come into conflict with my own. What's a half hour spent putting on shoes and socks while Mom waits, when you have a whole day ahead of you? Foolishly, I try to impart to them a sense of urgency.

I tell them of the many things I need to accomplish today. I remind them if we don't get going, there will be no time left for other activities they want to do. This doesn't faze them . . . until all of a sudden we are out of time. Then they cry because they missed a favorite TV show or can't go to the park.

Now that my son is older, however, he is beginning to echo back to me what I have said so many times in the past about the scarcity of time. The funny thing is, it makes me sad to hear him because it means he is losing something important. For kid-time is closer to God-time than adult-time is.

"He made from one the whole human race to dwell on the entire surface of the earth, and he fixed the ordered seasons and the boundaries of their regions, so that people might seek God, even perhaps grope for him and find him, though indeed he is not far from any one of us."
Acts 17:26-27

There'll Be Time Tomorrow

My copy of my parents' living will came in the mail today. It instructs me on what to do if they become unable to make life and death decisions for themselves.

I don't want to read it. How can they know now what they would want when and if? How can they sit in the comfort of their home and make decisions that will have to be carried out by me in the cold of an anonymous hospital? I'm not ready for this. I don't want to face this moral dilemma of our aging society. To die with dignity—that's all they want. That's all any of us want.

Still, I'll read their living will tomorrow. There'll be time tomorrow.

Seventy is the sum of our years, /or eighty, if we are strong. Ps 90:10

Family Meetings

Time for the ritual of the family meeting. It is a benevolent dictatorship that we run, my spouse and I. We give our children the illusion of letting them speak their piece.

We gather in a selected spot, like king and queen holding court, and allow our subjects to state their grievances. We listen calmly, then render our royal decision.

Lately, though, our kids have been turning the tables on us, once again shaking our grasp of power. Somehow, they have been getting their way! My husband and I end up playing scullery maid and court jester to their royal eminences. Our subjects have authored an insurrection. We have been banished to the dungeon while they plot our demise.

But, from the dungeon, we engineer our ascent back to power.

So much for being benevolent.

"You shall appoint judges and officials throughout your tribes to administer true justice for the people in the communities which the Lord, *your God, is giving you."*   *Dt 16:18*

Blame-Shifting

An awful lot of shifting of blame goes on in my home. He did this. She did that. They made me do it. Even at their young ages, my children already know that if they can just shift the blame to someone else, they may be able to weasel their way out of a punishment or reprimand.

There is no one as good at shifting blame as alcoholics and other addicts. They can convince even themselves that their problems are not their fault but rather are inflicted by a variety of nefarious causes and people. They have refined their system of placing blame so well that there is no reasoning with them.

What about us mothers? Do we accept responsibility for our own actions, or are we just as quick to shift the blame whenever and on whomever we can? The schools are no good, television is a wasteland, society is corrupt . . . we come from a dysfunctional family, our parents were divorced, the church doesn't help, no one taught us how to be a mother . . . .

There's enough blame being shifted around to cause an avalanche.

"Alas, we are being punished because of our brother." Gn 42:21

Inadequate?

Why is it we mothers are born inadequate? It is our fate. No matter how we try, we can never quite achieve complete competence. Even more foolishly, we strive to be more than competent, only to trip over our inadequacies over and over again.

The reason is that motherhood is an impossible job. No one can do it the way it should be done. That would mean being smarter, more patient, more holy than we are. (OK, maybe Jesus' mother Mary was adequate, but she had an only child—and besides, even she lost her kid for three whole days!)

Fortunately, adequate or not, we are the ones our children want as their mothers. Despite what we may think and they might say, they would not be happier with someone else. All they want from us is that we love them, keep them safe and warm and well-fed, and let them go when the time comes. If we do that, we will be adequate.

"But whoever enters through the gate is the shepherd of the sheep. The gate keeper opens it for him, and the sheep hear his voice, as he calls his own sheep by name and leads them out. When he has driven out all his own, he walks ahead of them and the sheep follow him, because they recognize his voice. But they will not follow a stranger; they will run away from him, because they do not recognize the voice of strangers." Jn 10:2-5

Make your bed. Brush your teeth.

    Hurry, you're late.

Eat your breakfast. Wash your face.

    Hurry, you're late.

Finish your breakfast. Comb your hair.

    Hurry, you're late.

Get your books. Grab your lunch.

    Hurry, you're late.

Here's the bus. Zip your jacket.

    Hurry, you're late.

Out the door. Here's a kiss.

    Hurry, you're . . . late.

"Look kindly on the prayer and petition of your servant, O Lord, my God, and listen to the cry of supplication which I, your servant, utter before you this day." 1 Kgs 8:28

Beaming

My youngest son came home beaming. He had scored a hundred percent on his first spelling quiz. You could see the pride in his strut. He had worked hard and succeeded. Isn't it amazing how little it takes to make him happy!

My oldest son also came home beaming today. He had made first string on the J.V. football team. He was pleasant to his siblings, and even offered to mow the lawn without my nagging! He had worked hard. He deserved his victory.

I'm beaming today, too. I received a momentary payback for my years of mothering. You'd think I had just landed a promotion or a movie contract. But, after all, I've worked hard. I deserve this moment of pride.

May our sons be like plants /well nurtured from their youth, /Our daughters, like carved columns, /shapely as those of the temple.
Ps 144:12

Runaway Mother

There goes another one. You can see it on her guilt-ridden face. You can see it in her anxious pacing to and fro, like a caged animal. It's a mother preparing to run.

She's had it with too much self-sacrifice, too much denial, too many demands. She's ready to bolt like a young colt straining under the training bridle. She pulls and pulls. She will not be broken. She's ready to leap the fence. Anyone who looks can see it in her eyes.

Except her family. They are blind.

There's still hope. Free-spirits can learn to live happily within domesticity. They are trainable, but they need freedom and respect. They need understanding spouses and children able to take some responsibility for themselves.

They need to be loved.

My soul is deprived of peace, /I have forgotten what happiness is; /I tell myself my future is lost, /all that I hoped for from the LORD.
Lam 3:17-18

The Tortoise and the Hare

Slow and steady wins the race. That's the wisdom of the story of the tortoise and the hare. But sometimes this can be so frustrating. I'd rather be the rabbit—with quick starts, darting here and there, frittering away time and energy, than the turtle—slowly plodding on, eyes on the goal, no effort wasted.

So I often appear to be scattered, distracted, off base. I expend a lot of energy on things that don't matter or end up fruitless. It drives my family nuts.

But what if I set one goal and plod after it, only to discover once there that it was not all it was cracked up to be? What if I spend my whole life pursuing one prize and miss all the others around me on the way?

Good turtles have tunnel-vision. I'd rather see far and wide like the rabbit—even if I do come in second.

Thus I do not run aimlessly; I do not fight as if I were shadow boxing. No, I drive my body and train it, for fear that, after having preached to others, I myself should be disqualified.
1 Cor 9:26-27

Self Care

"I'm much too tired and burdened to have any time for you." That's the silent message I often give my children without realizing it. They just read my body language and leave me alone.

What am I doing? These non-verbal signals don't work with the people I need to turn off. They just continue to press on with their demands. It does work with those I most want to say yes to—my family. But they are the ones who no longer ask, for fear of adding to my burdens.

I need to say "no" loudly and clearly to others, so I can say "yes" silently to the ones I love.

"Let your 'Yes' mean 'Yes,' and your 'No' mean 'No.' Anything more is from the evil one."
Mt 5:37

Frozen for Eternity

Further growing up is not allowed. My children have reached that magical age I want them to remain forever. They are old enough to dress and do a few other things for themselves, but young enough to still idolize their mom. What a wonderful, delightful age!

What's more, if they don't get any older, I won't get any older. I like the age I'm at, too. Let me live here forever, Lord. These are my golden years. I want to hold on to them.

To hug my own children who still fit in my lap and welcome those hugs—I've waited all of my life for this. I don't want to lose it.

I want to be frozen here for eternity!

Raise your eyes and look about; /they all gather and come to you: /Your sons come from afar, /and your daughters in the arms of their nurses. /Then you shall be radiant at what you see, /your heart shall throb and overflow, /For the riches of the sea shall be emptied out before you, /the wealth of nations shall be brought to you. Is 60:4-5

Church Alone

I almost feel guilty. Slipping off to church, leaving my husband with the kids so that tomorrow he might have the same blessing. The words of the homily never rang truer. I never sang quite so loudly. The prayers of thanksgiving echo in my soul, reverberating and renewing my spirit. Such deep solitude and community all at once!

In the pew in front of me two pre-schoolers squirm. I watch in sympathy as the mother tries to control them. In glee I smile at them and make faces.

I almost miss my own children.

Almost.

Send your light and fidelity, /that they may be my guide /And bring me to your holy mountain, /to the place of your dwelling, /That I may come to the altar of God, /to God, my joy, my delight. Ps 43:3-4

Hot Flashes

A rush of heat, sweat. I feel my face flush. Discretely, I remove my jacket. This has no relationship to the weather outside. It has everything to do with the weather inside. Inside of me, a storm rages. A hurricane. A tropical storm. Hot flashes, then chills. Blazes of irrationality. Rushes of hormones.

Change of life, they call it. It's a physical affliction I must endure—the same as I did those monthly cramps and the bloating and tension of PMS. I've been putting up with this body all of my life. Now it's time to speak out, to complain, to be a bitch. I've earned it. I have a right to it, after too many years of smiling when I felt like cursing. I'm too old to keep up the pretense any longer.

They say I'll get over it. (Who are "they," anyway?) They tell my husband to be patient—that I'll be the sweet, loving, long-suffering wife he always knew once again. Well, I'll see about that!

In the meantime I remove another layer of clothing. A layer of my life is being removed, and it scares me.

Cycles of years, positions of stars, /natures of animals, tempers of beasts, /Powers of the winds and thoughts of men, /uses of plants and virtues of roots— /Such things as are hidden I learned.
Wis 7:19-21

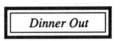

Dinner Out

It's been so long since I've eaten a meal I haven't prepared (or at least haven't defrosted and served), so long since I've sat at a table and been waited on rather than waited on others. My husband has to hold me down to keep me from getting up and helping the waiter get food off his cart. Each time someone calls for the waiter, I want to answer "just a minute."

My husband and I look at each other, we talk—actual adult communication. I smile and settle down, thinking I might start to like this. I realize that there is nothing to do but sit and eat. No jumping up for forgotten items or to clean up spilled milk, no telephone interruptions, no television in the background.

I cut into my steak, pop it in my mouth, and experience an amazing sensation.

"This food is hot!"

Wisdom has built her house, /she has set up her seven columns; She has dressed her meat, mixed her wine, /yes, she has spread her table.
Prv 9:1-2

Substitute Mother

When the student is ready, the teacher will come. (Chinese proverb)

I come each day to the same classroom, but I wonder if my students are really ready. They look at me, some with groggy, sleepfilled eyes; others with eager expectations, anticipating whatever wisdom I may have to impart. I try to guide their young minds—so like those of my own children—but I'm fighting so many losing battles. Some come to school hungry. Some from broken homes. Some from homes with no discipline. I end up being a disciplinarian, a social worker, a nurse, and a substitute mother, more than a teacher.

Yet I am learning so much from these children. So much about the reality of their young lives.

Your student is ready, Lord. Teach me.

So you, my child, be strong in the grace that is in Christ Jesus. And what you have heard from me through many witnesses entrust to faithful people who have the ability to teach others as well. 2 Tm 2:1-2

The Epidemic

There's an epidemic raging in our society. No family is safe from it, and all families are being affected in some way.

In a society where this disease rages, even good marriages are thrown away. It's become easier to divorce than to stay together and work through problems.

Now, there is no way to divorce-proof a marriage. No amount of candle-lit dinners, romantic getaways, or great sex can do it.

There is, however, one thing that can help. It is the children. They are the constant, physical incarnations of the love between husband and wife. And they need both their mom and dad, if at all possible.

Then the wolf shall be a guest of the lamb, /and the leopard shall lie down with the kid; /the calf and the young lion shall browse together, /with a little child to guide them. Is 11:6

Momaholic

She's not even employed, yet she's a work-aholic! Her children, her home, her volunteer activities: those are her jobs, and she's intense about all of them.

Even when she "plays" with her children, she's not really playing, she's working—working at being a good mother. She plays games intensely, bent not on winning but on teaching her kids how to win. She tolerates no fooling around. There is likewise no horse play when she's reading books to them. After all, reading is serious business!

She takes her volunteer positions very seriously, too. And her house—why house cleaning is one of her sacred tasks. Even preparing for Christmas is a major job to be done.

She schedules personal time for herself, doling it out in small portions because she can only handle so much before again feeling the need to be productive, to get things done. Even the time she allots to her spouse is justified on the basis of "building their relationship."

There's no workaholic worse than a momaholic.

I said to myself, "Come, now, let me try you with pleasure and the enjoyment of good things." But, behold, this too was vanity. Of laughter I said: "Mad!" and of mirth: "What good does this do?" Eccl 2:1-2

Romance

I want my children to experience romance. Not the romance of the mysterious stranger, but the romance of committed love with your best friend.

The romance of hands held while waiting for your first child to be born.

The romance of candle-lit dinners with a baby lying close by, interrupting your meal with gurgles—or even cries.

The romance of drives together to the emergency room with an injured child, and the romance of relief when the child recovers.

The romance of arguments and making up.

The romance of a lifetime together and memories to share.

I want my children to have the kind of romance I have had.

Love is patient, love is kind. It is not jealous, [love] is not pompous, it is not inflated, it is not rude, it does not seek its own interests, it is not quick-tempered, it does not brood over injury, it does not rejoice over wrongdoing, but rejoices with the truth. 1 Cor 13:4-6

Whining

"Whining doesn't work around here," I tell my kids. But it does and they know it. From the moment they get up until the moment they go to bed, life seems one constant whine. It's like an irritating hum or high pitched buzz that never completely goes away. Sometimes whining actually breaks out into a fight, but then it subsides back to low-level, irritating background noise.

I complain to my spouse when he gets home. I complain to God, to friends and family. I complain to strangers on the street.

"Ah, quit your whining," they tell me.

Then Moses said to Aaron, "Tell the whole Israelite community: Present yourselves before the LORD, for he has heard your grumbling."
Ex 16:9

> *Sins of the Mothers*

The sins of the fathers are visited upon the children, or so the Bible says. We mothers get off easy, don't we? Not so. The sins of the mothers are also visited on their children.

Children are very sensitive to their mother's actions and moods. In some ways, they know us better than we know ourselves. They closely observe how we deal with them and with other people. They see through our falsehoods and hypocrisies better than a magic mirror.

Without even knowing it, children pick up their mother's frustrated dreams, her hidden hurts—which become their dreams, their hurts. There is no way to entirely avoid this, because these are processes that happen without our awareness—or theirs.

All we mothers can do is keep our sins to a minimum, admit them to ourselves, and ask forgiveness of our children . . . and our God.

He said to her, "Your sins are forgiven." The others at table said to themselves, "Who is this who even forgives sins?" But he said to the woman, "Your faith has saved you; go in peace." Lk 7:48-50

> *Everybody Lies*

Everybody lies. We lie to be polite. We lie to save face, to avoid embarassment. We lie to avoid punishment or blame. We lie to see if we can get away with it. And most of all, we lie to ourselves. Everybody else sees it, but we're the last to face the truth about ourselves.

Our children on the other hand, can be brutal in their honesty.

"That's ugly, Mom."

"That man's fat!"

Our job is to teach our kids how to tell the truth without hurting others.

Stop lying to one another, since you have taken off the old self with its practices and have put on the new self, which is being renewed, for knowledge, in the image of its creator.
Col 3:9-10

Threatened

Why do I suddenly feel animosity towards this new mother? Why do I pick at everything she does and try to downplay her accomplishments? Why do I feel so threatened?

The answer is simple: she is younger than I. She has talents I didn't have, as hard as it is to admit this. Will my successes pale before hers? Will my years of experience and service count as nothing? Will she be a better mother?

I could be jealous, insist on competing with her, undercut her whenever possible. Or I could work with her, give her the benefit of my years of experience, be her mentor.

Am I strong enough in my own self-worth as a mother to do this? What if she uses what I teach her to step over me, or step on me?

Am I strong enough even for that?

Anger is relentless, and, wrath overwhelming—
/but before jealousy who can stand? Prv 27:4

Over-Extended

Over-extended. That's the name of my game. That's how I live my life.

What's one more kid to watch? One more meeting to attend? One more errand to run? When you're doing so much already, what's a little more? One more rung added to my extension ladder. I give a yank, pull on the halyard, and out goes one more extension reaching to the sky. It's wobbly though, that ladder.

I am over-extended not from an inability to say no, but from an overpowering desire to say yes! Yes, yes, yes! Not only do I say yes when asked, I seek out new areas to be involved in, areas of need either for myself, my children, or other people.

And when my ladder shakes and wobbles, I lean it against my firm foundation—my God.

I love you, LORD, my strength, /LORD, my rock, my fortress, my deliverer, /My God, my rock of refuge, /my shield, my saving horn, my stronghold! Ps 18:2-3

Living Together

There are two towering old fir trees in our backyard. When we first moved here, there were numerous dead branches hanging amidst the live ones, and one tree had a large gash in its trunk. But after consulting our local horticulturalist, I was reassured not only that our trees were healthy, but that I didn't need to prune away the dead branches. "They will fall away naturally over time," he said. "It's best just to leave them alone."

So, while I periodically trim back the bushes that try to overtake our yard, I have resisted the temptation to knock down the dead branches from our fir trees. It's only now, three years later, that I have begun to truly appreciate the beauty of those trees.

In our society, we cover over death with make-up and flowers. We are quick to pluck the dying flower or the gray hair. We hide from the unpleasant realities of death because we haven't learned the lesson of the fir tree. We don't see the beauty of old, dying branches mixed with young, living ones. We don't allow for the reality of pain mixed with pleasure. We want only happy thoughts and nice days rather than the contradiction of joy and sorrow side by side.

Listen to the wisdom of the fir tree, mother. See the beauty of old and young, all of us in different stages of new birth and dying, living together.

Gray hair is a crown of glory; /it is gained by virtuous living. Prv 16:31

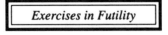

Exercises in Futility

Folding laundry before putting it in children's drawers.

Tying children's shoes.

Telling children to tie their shoes.

Telling children to pick up their rooms.

Picking up children's rooms.

Asking children to do just about anything.

Bit by bit, like the drop of water on a stone, these exercises in futility wear you away.

No wonder mothers get smaller as we age. We aren't really shrinking, we are being beaten down.

Four things are among the smallest on the earth, /and yet are exceedingly wise.
Prv 30:24

Caught between Two Worlds

Mom. It's me, your daughter. I'm fifteen years old, and yet I feel like I'm no better at communicating with you than when I was a baby. Sometimes I long to crawl into your arms and feel safe again, but something in me resists, refuses to give in. I'm afraid to do so would make me a child forever. I'm afraid you would hold me too hard.

I'm caught between two worlds, Mom. I can't return to the old one—I've outgrown it. But I'm not ready for the new. I want to be over with this waiting, this ambivalence.

Mom, help me move between those two worlds. Just let me come to you, and let me go.

———————————

"Our sister is little, /and she has no breasts as yet. /What shall we do for our sister /when her courtship begins? /If she is a wall, /we will build upon it a silver parapet; /If she is a door, /we will reinforce it with a cedar plank. Song 8:8-9

"I Do"

She wipes the drool from the corner of her husband's mouth and encourages him to feed himself. One side of his face droops, like an imprint on silly putty pulled slightly down. With his good side he looks at her and she sees her best friend. She smiles and reassures him that everything will be fine. He looks at her blankly, and yet full of trust.

He struggles to bring the spoon to his mouth. She resists the urge to help him. She knows this is a battle he must wage himself.

Still, she is with him every minute during his therapy as they try to re-teach him how to talk, how to walk. Their kids come to visit, then go back to their own lives, but she stays with him always.

That's what she promised when she said, "I do."

So faith, hope, love remain, these three; but the greatest of these is love. 1 Cor 13:13

The Good Father

The only illusion as hard to let go of as that of the Good Mother is that of the Good Father. No man can live up to the role of the perfect dad, and so our spouses are as doomed to failure as we.

Still, fathers are a safety valve against a mother's blind spots, her inability to see the harm she may be doing unknowingly to her children. Without them, we'd be totally on our own.

Thank you, Father, for fathers . . . imperfect though they are.

I am writing to you, fathers, because you know him who is from the beginning. 1 Jn 2:13

A Disparaging Word

Mother, watch that tongue. Your words are swords that cut both ways, for good or for evil. Young ears are sensitive to name-calling and disparaging words that attack their fragile sense of self. Your condemnations cut to the quick.

So shout if you're angry, yell if you must, but guard against words that destroy your very own children.

Once spoken, they cannot be recalled.

Indeed, the word of God is living and effective, sharper than any two-edged sword, penetrating even between soul and spirit, joints and marrow, and able to discern reflections and thoughts of the heart. Heb 4:12

First Grade

Some days my son comes home from school ready to snap. We end up in an argument over the smallest thing, and he gets sent to his room for a cooling off period. His adjustment from kindergarten to first grade is harder than I had expected.

It's hard for me to imagine the world my son lives in. I see it as playing with blocks, running during recess, and making new friends.

It seems to him more like a pressure tank, though—all those young bodies pressed into one space ready to explode, forced to learn how to relate to each other; the name calling, the peer pressure, the ostracism; the pressure to achieve, to learn to read, to take tests, to do homework. No wonder my son is irritable at the end of the day.

What happened to the sweet picture of school he had last year?

Gone in the face of the reality of first grade!

I rejoice greatly in the Lord that now at last you revived your concern for me. You were, of course, concerned about me but lacked an opportunity. Not that I say this because of need, for I have learned, in whatever situation I find myself, to be self-sufficient. Phil 4:10-11

Empty Nest

What is all this talk about an empty nest syndrome? My nest has never been so full. My little fledglings, whom I had successfully launched to college and careers, have all returned home to a nest they've long ago outgrown.

Our home, which comfortably managed to hold two adults and four children, and which even sufficed through the teen years, was not made to hold six adults. It can stretch no more. To do so would destroy its elasticity for all time and may very well destroy what should be a blooming friendship with our now-adult children.

Maybe my spouse and I should abdicate, turn over the keys, and get while the getting's still good. We'll leave the house to our children—just before the furnace breaks down for the final time, when the refrigerator's on its last legs, and while there's still some material left on our faded furniture.

We'll abandon the nest and fly south until our children finally do the decent thing and allow us our empty nest! We earned it and we deserve it.

And you shall know that your tent is secure;
/taking stock of your household, you shall miss
nothing. /You shall know that your descendants
are many, /and your offspring as the grass of the
earth. Jb 5:24-25

Widow

Will the numbness ever end? She wants it to end and yet she fears it will. As long as she is numb, she doesn't have to feel. As long as she doesn't feel, she doesn't have to hurt. She can walk around in unreality, believing it's not true, waiting for him to come home.

She's so glad the funeral is over. The mourners have gone back to their own lives, but she has got to build a new life. Hers has been permanently changed, more permanently than even the day, thirty-one years ago, when they were married. Then a bond was formed. Now the bond has been ripped apart, beyond repair.

So many of her friends have been through this. How unfeeling she had been to their pain! Now they come forward as the ones who know and they comfort her. Those who don't know are as unfeeling as she once was—not out of unkindness, just out of ignorance. She forgives them, but please don't tell her to get on with it. She can't just yet. She's not ready to accept the title "widow."

"In my father's house there are many dwelling places. If there were not, would I have told you that I am going to prepare a place for you? And if I go and prepare a place for you, I will come back again and take you to myself, so that where I am you also may be." Jn 14:2-3

Tattle-Tales

"Mom, guess who got in trouble at school today?" my daughter asks.

"Mom, she told me to do it," my son interrupts.

He did, she said. Back and forth tattle-tales. The end result is total confusion, when what I want is honest communication.

He said, she did.

The muddier the water gets, the less I want to dive in.

For every kind of beast and bird, of reptile and sea creature, can be tamed and has been tamed by the human species, but no human being can tame the tongue. Jas 3:7

In Darkness

It is the middle of the night—this mother's favorite time. I am safe and secure. No one bothers me. My family allows me to be alone with my thoughts. I let my dreams play with each other. My fantasies run free. My tears flow. I smile. I laugh out loud. So much seems possible while in darkness.

Darkness is kind and accepting. It hides my failings, forgives me my faults. It whispers its love and wraps me in its warmth. It allows me my feelings—the whole wide range. It makes no demands. It sweeps away responsibilities. Let them wait until morning.

In darkness I wait. I find healing and acceptance there.

In darkness I encounter my God.

I will give you treasures out of the darkness, /and riches that have been hidden away, /That you may know that I am the LORD, /the God of Israel, who calls you by your name. Is 45:3

A Dead Bird

"Mommy, lookit," my daughter says through her tears. She brings in the bird caught by our intrepid cat. "Can you fix it?"

No, it's time she learns. Mom can't fix everything, can't cure every hurt or change the inevitable.

We bury the bird in the backyard and my daughter goes back to her play, seemingly unaffected, seeming to have forgotten the whole affair. It's I whom this incident preys upon, who keeps reliving the picture of the small child with the small bird, my own powerlessness in the face of tragedy and death.

Somehow, I feel that I let her down.

"Are not two sparrows sold for a small coin? Yet not one of them falls to the ground without your Father's knowledge." Mt 10:29

Day Care Crunch

Another scandal in day care: a child forgotten; a child abused. What's a working mother to do?

No woman can work well if she's worried about her children, but where does she draw the line? Quality day care is so hard to find. For every dollar she makes she pays thirty cents in day care costs. Is she being too picky? Over-protective? She can't afford to pay the providers what they are really worth, yet she can't afford to be without child care. So she reassures herself that her children are OK.

And then another scandal in day care appears in the paper.

Crowd upon crowd /in the valley of decision;
/For near is the day of the LORD /in the valley of
decision. Jl 4:14

Mentor

The Bible tells so much about Ruth's faithfulness to her mother-in-law, but so little about the critical role Naomi played.

What was it about Naomi that attracted Ruth to her? Naomi was more than a mother-in-law to Ruth. She was a spiritual mother, a mentor teaching Ruth to love a new God, Yahweh.

Women are not raised to value mentor relationships. Yet most men realize how needed and necessary they are. Why are spiritual mothers so hard to find, and so poorly recognized when they are?

Ruth went home to her mother-in-law, who asked, "How have you fared, my daughter" So she told her all the man had done for her, and concluded, "He gave me these six measures of barley because he did not wish me to come back to my mother-in-law empty handed!' " Naomi then said, "Wait here, my daughter, until you learn what happens, for the man will not rest, but will settle the matter today." Ru 3:16-18

Make-up

My daughters watch as I put on my make-up.

"Can I have some, Mommy?" they ask. I stop long enough to splash a little blush on their cheeks.

Cosmetics are part of the ritual of femininity. My daughters are curious about this aspect of the adult world. They role-play in preparation for their own debut. They await their entry into the world of glamour.

And it is I who must open the door for them.

———————————————

Ah, you are beautiful, my beloved, /ah, you are beautiful! Song 4:1

Computer World

Today's newest frontier is information technology. Computers are expanding our ability to collect and process information at a rate never conceived by our parents.

How will this rapid growth and exchange of knowledge affect the next generation? Are we in danger of overloading and short-circuiting our children?

Mothers are natural limit setters. How do we set limits on knowledge?

If I have the gift of prophesy and comprehend all mysteries and all knowledge; if I have all faith so as to move mountains but do not have love, I am nothing. 1 Cor 13:2

God's Will

There's this mysterious concept out there called "God's will." We don't know exactly what it is, but we mothers invoke it repeatedly. When tragedy strikes—it's God's will. When we plan to do something—we'll do it, God willing. When we finally decide what to do with our lives—it's God's calling.

In truth, isn't "God's will" just another way of shifting responsibility off our shoulders and onto God's? Invoking God's will gives mothers grandiose power and authority: "It's God's will that I do this, and you better get out of my way or God will get you." "I'm only doing this for you." "I'm only doing this for God." "I have no self-interest involved."

All mothers know the lie of that.

What would be so wrong with saying, "I willed this and I hope it's OK with God"? or "I'm doing this for myself, for my own reasons, and I hope others will benefit also"? Why is it that God's will and our own wills have to be seen as diametrically opposed?

Isn't it quite possible that sometimes, just maybe, God might will for us what we will for ourselves?

Say not: "It was God's doing that I fell away";
/for what he hates he does not do. Sir 15:11

Ogling Women

It's a known fact that some men ogle women. Men's magazines even have articles on how to perfect this skill—as if men needed any help! Men learn at an early age how to undress women with their eyes. Some are quite subtle, some are quite blatant, but most do it to a greater or lesser degree. They do it for the pleasure it gives them.

It's also known that some women ogle other women. We don't undress them, but we do size them up and tear them apart. We note hair color and style and whether it's natural or dyed. We notice make-up or lack thereof. We check out clothing and shoes and accessories—whether they all match, whether they compliment the wearer or accent a big nose or bulging thighs. We do it for comparison purposes, to see how we are doing *vis a vis* the competition.

Men and women both ogle women, but for different reasons.

Which are worse?

We hear that some are conducting themselves among you in a disorderly way, by not keeping busy but minding the business of others. Such people we instruct and urge in the Lord Jesus Christ to work quietly and to eat their own food. 2 Thes 3:11-12

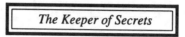

The Keeper of Secrets

Keeping another person's life in order. Typing letters, filing papers, ordering supplies, attending to the many details of office life. Secretary . . . the keeper of secrets.

When anything goes wrong, she's the first to be blamed. So much easier for her boss to say, "I'll have my secretary check into it," or "my secretary must have misplaced it," than to admit a mistake. She accepts the blame to make her boss look good.

Everyone who knows anything about business knows that the boss is only as good as his or her secretary. She makes or breaks the boss.

It's amazing how much good mothers are like good secretaries.

Greet Prisca and Aquila, my co-workers in Christ Jesus, who risked their necks for my life, to whom not only I am grateful but also all the churches of the Gentiles. Rom 16:3

Trash

They called her trash. Her husband was the town alcoholic. He would come home just long enough to get her pregnant, then go off on another binge. She lived on the wrong side of the tracks, and everybody knew she was a bad mother.

So she left the town and started over. She got her life back together. Her children grew up to be productive members of society. But whenever she came home, she was still trash in the eyes of the townspeople.

They could not see her beauty.

Jesus said to them, "A prophet is not without honor except in his native place and among his own kin and in his own house." Mk 6:4

Self-Destruction

My daughter has started down the road to self-destruction once again. There is no reasoning with her, no pointing out to her what she is doing. Any attempt to do so just fans the flames of her tantrum. To threaten loss of privileges does no good. She has been told that many times to no avail. The immediate manifestation of anger and rage seem too necessary to her right now. So I sit out the tantrum, and when she's finished we talk.

My daughter is only four. I can set limits around her now to protect her from herself. But who will protect her from herself when she is twenty-four?

Only you, my God.

Jesus spoke to them again, saying, "I am the light of the world. Whoever follows me will not walk in darkness, but will have the light of life."
Jn 8:12

Baby Dance

baby surges, baby urges

    in my womb

kick, giggle, gasp

    baby dance

        in my womb

who is this person

    swimming from the end of an umbilical cord

bouncing off a soft inner wall

    mother-child in a symbiotic dance

my life depends on you,

    your life depends on me,

        we need each other, child

baby suckling, tugging at mama's breast

    we need each other, child

in a way never known,

    and always known

        we need each other

---

*Can a mother forget her infant, /be without
tenderness for the child of her womb?
Is 49:15*

Chicken Pox

A pox on the pox! This is a childhood disease, only now catching up to me as an adult! I thought I had escaped the chicken pox, only to be hit with its full fearsome force now that I'm grown.

There's something to be said for experiencing all things in their due time. The time to have chicken pox is when you are young. To have to suffer through it as an adult is almost unbearable.

Likewise, the time to go through adolescence is the teen years. To have to deal with adolescent issues as an adult is unbecoming and embarrassing. And yet there are those of us who have to do so. We have to go back to resolve some difficult crisis of childhood.

We can't bypass any of life's rites of passage, any of the normal pains of growing up. If we try to, they'll catch up to us eventually. Childhood crises are best dealt with while still a child, before adding the stress and responsibility of adulthood. But deal with them we must.

Thus says the LORD: /Let not the wise man glory in his wisdom, /nor the strong man glory in his strength, /nor the rich man glory in his riches. Jer 9:22

Planning for Retirement

We mothers have to start today to plan for our retirement years—not by acquiring stocks and bonds, but by acquiring grace and love.

Will we become old and bitter with an ever narrower world view, or age with wisdom and dignity?

Look at the old ladies around you. Like which ones do you want to become? Start planning now.

There was also a prophetess, Anna, the daughter of Phanuel, of the tribe of Asher. She was advanced in years, having lived seven years with her husband after her marriage, and then as a widow until she was eighty-four . . . . And coming forward at that very time, she gave thanks to God and spoke about the child to all who were awaiting the redemption of Jerusalem. Lk 2:36-38

If I Were a Bird

I'm taking my cues from the birds that fly south. They know better than to wait and get caught in the snow and ice. They know when to leave.

But then, they don't have a home to worry about. They don't have to pack bags or transfer children to a new school system. They have only their feathers to keep them warm, and that is all they need. Their young are out of the nests by the end of summer.

Life would be so much simpler if only I were a bird. But, since I'm not, it's time to get out the longjohns and thermal shirts, time to batten down the hatches and prepare for another winter.

Maybe some day I'll be as free as the birds. Until then, I'm a mother.

What are these that fly along like clouds, /like doves to their cotes? Is 60:8

Witch Mom, Part 2

"Grrr," the alarm goes off. I roll over in bed.

"Mom, it's time to get up," little voices echo.

I growl and crawl out of bed. "Out of my way!"

"Oh, no, it's Witch Mom," my kids whisper. They know what this means. No fighting, no complaining, no talking above a whisper. My children scurry to and fro, speaking softly while I fumble for a cup of coffee.

My youngest dares to speak, "Mom, how come you never buy sugar cereal?" she whines. Her siblings caution her to be silent, but it's too late.

"What's that?!" I turn and snap. "Who dares to talk to Witch Mom?" I raise my hand to cast a spell.

"She didn't mean it, Mother, really," my oldest intervenes. I stare at him and head for the sofa while they clear their dishes and hurry to get dressed.

I send them off to school with a quick kiss and another growl. The whole procedure took only half an hour.

The Good Mother may be better liked, but Witch Mom gets results!

Do everything without grumbling or question-
ing, that you may be blameless and innocent,
children of God without blemish in the midst of
a crooked and perverse generation, among
whom you shine like lights in the world.
Phil 2:14

Lonely

Loneliness is an inescapable human reality. Nothing can completely fill the void that is inside of all of us. Not our spouses. Not our children. Not our grandchildren, or their children.

Only God can fill us up.

Then he made the disciples get into the boat and precede him to the other side, while he dismissed the crowds. After doing so, he went up on the mountain by himself to pray. When it was evening he was there alone. _Mt 14:22-23_

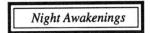

Night Awakenings

My daughter cries out softly in her sleep. I awaken immediately. I listen for her voice, but apparently she has fallen back asleep. I roll over and try to sleep.

Night awakenings. They are a regular part of my existence now. I toss. I turn. I fight to get back to sleep. Sometimes it comes, sometimes it doesn't. My mind rushes with thoughts: busy thoughts, anxious thoughts, troubled thoughts.

At night, I am inspired by ideas: some good, some bad. I've learned to be slow to trust these inspirations. Only in the light of day can I determine which were truly from God.

The people who walked in darkness /have seen a great light; /Upon those who dwelt in the land of gloom /a light has shone. Is 9:1

Mother Bear

Everyone knows not to get between a she-bear and her cubs. She will kill to protect her children.

Never get between me and my children, either. I would die for them. Instinct would set in where reason left off.

So beware.

Hear me, O house of Jacob, /all who remain of the house of Israel, /My burden since your birth, /whom I have carried from your infancy. /Even to your old age I am the same, /even when your hair is gray I will bear you. Is 46:3-4

Welcome Back

It's already time to unpack winter clothes that it seems I packed away only yesterday. I dread shutting windows and turning on the heat. I loathe the return of daily searches for boots and mittens and hats—and the constant reminders to the kids to wear them. I hate these autumn days of dressing for cold weather in the morning, only to come home sweating in the afternoon. I despise the inevitable fall colds as weather fluctuates erratically and children are cooped up once again with other children spreading germs.

Dread. Loathe. Hate. Despise.

Welcome back, Winter.

Have you entered the storehouse of the snow, /and seen the treasury of the hail /Which I have reserved for times of stress, /for the days of war and of battle? Jb 38:22-23

Leaves

I can remember as a child raking leaves and going over and over the same spot in search of perfection. I wanted to get every shred of leaf off that spot, leaving a space perfectly devoid of any debris.

"You don't have to get every leaf, Patty. Just get most of them," my mother would say in frustration. Luckily for her she had other children, or the job would never have been done.

Today, I sweep up the majority of leaves in my yard and let the rest blow into other people's yards as theirs blow into mine. I've learned a very valuable lesson since I've become a mother: not everything is worth doing, and not everything worth doing is worth doing well.

Instead, I do the best that I can with the tasks that lie before me each day. I prioritize rather than trying to do everything, and I find that—just like those leaves that blow into someone else's yard—sometimes the undone tasks miraculously disappear.

"Can any of you by worrying add a moment to your lifespan? If even the smallest things are beyond your control, why are you anxious about the rest?" Lk 12:25-26

Mom and Dad Fighting

Mom and Dad are fighting again. I can hear them even through my bedroom door. I don't want to listen. It frightens me.

My best friend's mom and dad are divorced. She only sees her dad on weekends now. She misses him. She says her parents used to fight a lot. She didn't like their fighting. Now they don't fight as much.

My friend gets two Christmases every year. One with her dad and one with her mom. She also gets two birthdays. It used to be when her dad came home from work he never paid her much attention. Now he plans special activities for their weekends together.

Still, she wishes her mom and dad would make up so they could be together again.

I don't want my mom and dad to divorce. I don't like to hear them fight. Maybe if I cover my head with my pillow and pretend it's not happening it will all go away. Maybe it will be better in the morning.

All bitterness, fury, anger, shouting, and reviling must be removed from you, along with all malice. [And] be kind to one another, compassionate, forgiving one another as God has forgiven you in Christ. Eph 4:31-32

Falling Illusions

The gentle breeze blows and those leaves that are ready fall to the ground, one by one, like rose petals covering the earth.

Then a harsh storm comes. The wind and the rain crash against the trees, shaking them fiercely, shaking loose all but the most stubborn leaves. Finally, just before winter, even those stubborn remainders fall, dying a natural death, resisting to the last.

A gentle breeze has been stripping me of my illusions. One by one they fall when they are ready. Then a storm arrives and forcibly picks me clean, until only the most stubborn remain, waiting their time to fall. Even those few have to go.

What will be left of me when all my illusions are gone?

We did not follow cleverly devised myths when we made known to you the power and coming of our Lord Jesus Christ, but we had been eyewitnesses of his majesty. 2 Pt 1:16

Alone

Her child is dying from the dreaded blood disease AIDS. How he got it she doesn't even want to know. He's been on his own for a long time, but now he's come home to die.

"We'll get through this," she tells him, just as she reassured him the night he struck out in the little league championship game.

"Not this time, Mom," he says. "You'll have to finish this one without me."

But she doesn't think she can do it. She can't make it through this thing by herself. Where are her other children? Where are her friends?

They stay away, afraid to be too close to the disease.

Day by day he gets weaker until she's no longer able to care for him.

He leaves home one last time, and she is alone— just as he predicted.

So we are always courageous, although we know that while we are at home in the body we are away from the Lord, for we walk by faith, not by sight. Yet we are courageous, and we would rather leave the body and go home to the Lord. 2 Cor 5:6-8

> *Empty*

I miss my former life. The one I used to have when my children were still young and at home. I never thought this day would come, but now I feel so alone. Alone in a house full of memories. Alone in a life too empty to fill. My life is over. The meaning is gone.

My husband says this is utter nonsense. Now we can finally do all the things we've wanted to do for so long but couldn't because of the children. We can finally run nude through the house and make love without worrying whether the bedroom door is locked. Take off to Tahiti or the Bahamas for a second honeymoon. Lie in bed and sip gourmet coffees and feast on fresh strawberries in sweet cream. Go away for a weekend on a whim and not have to worry about what state the house will be in when we return.

But all of these things pale in comparison to what I have lost: the noise, the clutter, the high food bills, the piles of laundry. I have lost my children.

Will anything ever fill this emptiness?

I consider the days of old; /the years long past I remember. /In the night I meditate in my heart; /I ponder and my spirit broods. Ps 77:6-7

Double Trouble

Sufficient unto themselves—that's what twins are.

My daughters are never really at a loss for playmates because they have each other—unlike their singleton brothers, who need and crave companionship and have to seek it at school, on the streets, in back-yards, and elsewhere.

Each of my girls also has a co-conspirator ready to come to her aid, speak for her, support her in her efforts to do what she wants. I can jump up and down, yell and scream, stand on my head—all to no avail. They don't take me seriously because they have little need for my approval. As long as their twin approves of what they are doing, who cares what Mommy thinks? Sufficient unto themselves. How do you get through to someone like that?

Answer: You don't and you don't.

Return, rebellious children /and I will cure you of your rebelling. Jer 3:22

To Plan and Dream Again

While my children are at school or day care, I think about the many unique moments I am missing. I worry about how they are doing. I realize just how precious and special they are. My thoughts turn to them throughout the day. I make plans for fun adventures to do together on my day off. I plan favorite meals and surprises and look forward to spending time with them. I count the minutes until they are home and wish that I didn't have to work and be away from them.

That's when they are at school or day care.

The minute I pick them up, I am barraged with demands and requests. They snarl at each other and before long all of us are snarling. One demands to go to a friend's house. The other wants ice cream or pizza. My well-laid plans go awry with the reality of their presence. The day ends in screaming fits as over-tired, wound-up children mix with over-tired, over-wrought parent. I can't wait until they are safely and quietly in bed and asleep.

Then I begin to plan and dream again.

"Then afterward I will pour out /my spirit upon all mankind. /Your sons and daughters shall prophesy, /your old men shall dream dreams, /your young men shall see visions." Jl 3:1

Translator

When in high school and studying French and Spanish, I used to dream of becoming a translator for the United Nations. There I'd be associating with political bigwigs, interpreting back and forth for them. Perhaps I could be a powerful force for peace by helping to translate world-wide peace negotiations.

Today I am in the translating business, only it isn't as glamorous as I had dreamed nor does it pay all that well. I'm busy translating for my kids. That grunt from the baby means "I've soiled my diaper;" that cry means "I'm hungry;" that scream means "big brother is bothering me."

As they get older, I still find myself translating— this time between my children and their teachers. "Here is what the teacher wants," or "What my daughter meant to say was . . . ." And now that my eldest is in his teen years, I'm learning a whole new language of slang and non-verbal communications.

Now, when the inevitable fights arise among my children I use my skills to negotiate for peace. Same dream, just a different setting.

They were astounded, and in amazement they asked, "Are not all these people who are speaking Galileans? Then how does each of us hear them in his own native language?"
Acts 2:7-8

Pets

"Mommy, can I please have a pet?"

"Later. We'll discuss this later. Maybe when you're old enough to take care of it yourself. Or when we buy a house in the country. You can't keep a pet cooped up in a house in the city, you know."

I've run out of pet excuses. I can't put off the inevitable much longer. Pets teach children about caring for living things and about taking responsibility—two of my favorite lessons.

Let's face it, for every reason to have a pet, there are ten reasons not to. Just as for every reason to have children, there are many more not to.

If I'm going to have children, I guess I'm going to have to have pets.

How varied are your works, Lord! /In wisdom you have wrought them all; /the earth is full of your creatures. Ps 104:24

Halloween

"Look, Mom, I wrote a story for Halloween."

"That's nice. Why not read it to me?"

"OK, but you'd better sit down. It's pretty scary.

"Two cars drove up to the cemetery on Halloween night. One guy stepped out. He said to the guy in the car, 'Aren't you going to come out?'

"'No, I'm going to stay in here,' he said.

"The guy walked down to the graveyard and he went down the hill where a lot of tombstones were. He saw an open grave. He looked at the grave and he heard a crash and a boom. Then it started to rain blood. He fell to the ground. A ghost appeared. It disappeared and the cross that used to be on the gravestone turned into a gun and a bomb and a knife. The ghost appeared again with one hand holding the knife. The other had the gun. He disappeared again, then two ghosts appeared. Then they disappeared again. Their grave started to light up. The other guy in the car heard the scream and drove all the way home. When he went home the whole town was lit up with ghosts and goblins. Then the whole town blew up to a ghost world. The End."

That kid watches way too much TV!

See to it that no one captivate you with an empty, seductive philosophy according to human tradition, according to the elemental powers of the world and not according to Christ. Col 2:8

The Mommy Game

Ever try to carry on three conversations at once? If you have, you are probably a mother. Your children ask you two things, your spouse asks another. And they wonder why you call them by the wrong names sometimes.

"Mom, I'm not Gwendolyn. Gwendolyn's the dog."

"Oh, you know what I mean. Don't confuse me with the facts."

"Honey, why did you put a note to the kid's teacher in my briefcase?"

"Shut up and let the dog in."

"Mom, that's Joey you just put outside, not the dog . . . ."

Incoherence, that's the name of the Mommy Game.

We have not received the spirit of the world but the Spirit that is from God, so that we may understand the things freely given us by God. And we speak about them not with words taught by human wisdom, but with words taught by the Spirit. 1 Cor 2:12-13

Contact

It's such a gray and gloomy day, I have to take time to say I love you. Even though you are far away from me now, my grief remains constant. I miss you.

Even though it's been twenty years, it seems like yesterday that you died, yesterday that you were alive. You are still so much a part of my life. Sometimes I see you, yet I know you're not there.

Come lie with me one more time, my husband. Hold me while I cry. We don't have to make love, I just want to make contact.

It's such a gray and gloomy day, I have to take time to say I love you.

For the Lord himself, with a word of command, with the voice of an archangel and with the trumpet of God, will come down from heaven, and the dead in Christ will rise first. Then we who are alive, who are left, will be caught up together with them in the clouds to meet the Lord in the air. 1 Thes 4:16-17

Mom's Sick

Mom's sick. Has the world come to an end? Has it temporarily stopped turning on its axis? Everything is out of whack because Mom is sick. Who will cook the meals? Who will do the laundry? Who will clean the house and get the kids off to school?

"Don't worry, dear," he says. "I'll take care of everything. I'll get the kids to school. I'll bring home pizza for supper tonight. You just stay in bed and rest."

Hushed voices downstairs, feet running here and there, doors slamming, they're gone. I go downstairs to assess the damage . . . .

Now I'm really sick.

Simon's mother-in-law was afflicted with a severe fever, and they interceded with him about her. He stood over her, rebuked the fever, and it left her. She got up immediately and waited on them. Lk 4:38-39

Pain

A life gone. Purposefully taken with his own hand. How long had he planned this? How many months of despair were hidden behind his distant eyes? He was her daughter's husband. He was the son she never had. And yet there was a pain that neither of them could reach. All their love couldn't make up for his hurt.

She holds her daughter close. They walk from the grave together, leaning on each other. They will continue to lean on each other for the rest of their lives.

How little we understand, those of us who've never experienced such a loss. No one says, "Now he's out of his pain," and yet he is—as surely as if he had been suffering from a painful illness all these years. Only he knew the extent of that pain.

Alone he found a solution to his pain.

Together his wife and her mother must find the strength to deal with theirs.

Why are you downcast, my soul, /why do you groan within me? /Wait for God, whom I shall praise again, /my savior and my God.
Ps 42:12

Grown Up

What do you want to be when you grow up? My children discuss this very important topic every now and then. A space doctor, one says. A rock star, another chooses. A police officer, nurse. Batman, my son proclaims.

What does it mean to be grown up? This is what I'd like to know. Does it mean having children and buying a house? Does it mean that everything in your life is settled? That you know what you are to do for the rest of your life? That there will be no more questions because all of the important ones have been answered?

Funny, I don't feel grown up.

It is not that I have already taken hold of it or have already attained perfect maturity, but I continue my pursuit in hope that I may possess it. Phil 3:12

Adopted

Her adopted son struggles with his identity. Much as she loves him, love isn't enough. There's a gap in his life, a missing link. He longs to know more about his biological parents.

He's an adult now, but it still pains her to see his struggle. She wonders, was he ever hers? Was this child who brought her so much joy as an infant, whom she cuddled and held and raised as her own, ever really hers? She feels so threatened and insecure at the thought of losing him to another mother. She is angry for the pain he is going through, angry at her own pain as she watches, helplessly, as he searches for his "real" mother.

Aren't we all adopted children in search of our heavenly parent? Don't all mothers suffer as they observe their children's lifelong search for happiness and completeness?

"Ask and it will be given to you; seek and you will find; knock and the door will be opened to you. For everyone who asks, receives; and the one who seeks, finds; and to the one who knocks, the door will be opened." Mt 7:7-8

Freedom from Shame

"Shame on you," she shakes her finger and points at the child. "Shame, shame," and in this manner the child is molded into obedience.

Ah, to be free of such shame. Is there a person alive who knows what it is to feel no shame? We term women "shameless hussies" who care little for what others think. Is it so bad to be that way—to be without the feeling that something is wrong with you unless you fit what society determines; that you are a mistake, not that you make mistakes?

I don't want my children's lives shame-filled. They may have wounds that need to be healed, but they are not flawed persons.

There is no shame in that.

"Whoever causes one of these little ones who believe in me to sin, it would be better for him if a great millstone were put around his neck and he were thrown into the sea." Mk 9:42

Best Laid Plans

The best laid plans of mice and . . . . Now wait a minute. Do you mean to tell me that mice make plans? Or men either, for that matter? I thought they were both wiser than that. It's we mothers who are crazy enough to be constantly making plans—only to have them thrown awry, constantly.

We plan our errands for the day, neatly calculating precisely how long it will take us to get from one place to the next, only to be thrown into a rage when stuck behind a man in a hat driving 35 in a 55 mile-per-hour, no passing zone. We plan family activities only to find the rest of the family doesn't buy them. Our idea of fun doesn't coincide with theirs. And, the most disastrous of all, we plan family vacations. Need I say more?

Still we continue to make plans for ourselves, our husbands, our children, our future. There is something within mothers that compels us to plan, and then gets furious when those plans don't work out.

Then again, there are those rare moments when our plans actually succeed.

These are enough to keep us planning into the next century!

How numerous, O LORD, my God, /you have made your wonderous deeds! /And in your plans for us /there is none to equal you.
Ps 40:6

Kids and Sex

Nothing kills the sex drive more quickly than a kid's half hour temper tantrum.

And no matter how sexy you might have felt during the day, the minute you walk in the door and are greeted by coats and backpacks thrown everywhere and children demanding food, you immediately became "Mom" again. And—let's face it—"moms" are not sexy.

On the other hand, nothing enhances sex more than sending all your children on an overnight some-where—anywhere—else.

Sheepfolds and orchards bring flourishing health; /but better than either, a devoted wife; /Wine and music delight the soul, /but better than either, conjugal love. Sir 40:19-20

Wounds

Like a hurt tigress, the wounded mother retreats to her lair to lick her wounds. She won't let anyone approach her. She snarls at those who dare. She won't let them see her cuts, no matter how deep.

She waits for time to heal her. But time alone can do only so much. This mother needs someone to clean out the infection she is unable to reach and to bind her wounds.

She needs a touch from the hands of the Healer.

Will she let such a One into her lair?

_____

"Do not let your hearts be troubled. You have faith in God; have faith also in me." Jn 14:1

Sleeping Beauty

Where are the adventurous tales of the struggle for good over evil by a strong, brave princess?

We women can no longer afford to sleepily await the arrival of our handsome prince. He may never come. We need to be active in the world around us, striving to bring good, to make a difference.

The world needs what women have to offer: a different model for leadership—one built on empowering each other in a circle, rather than climbing alone to the top.

Women can no longer afford to lie back passively, waiting for men to do all the work, to make us come alive, to give meaning to our lives. Our lives have meaning in and of themselves.

Awake, sleeping beauties of the world, awake!

"But the LORD Almighty thwarted them, /by a woman's hand he confounded them." Jdt 16:5

The Porch Swing, Part 2

The porch swing is the last thing to come in as winter draws near. I resist putting it away. Maybe there will be one more nice fall day, one more opportunity to sit peacefully with the sun in my face. But I pull my jacket more tightly around me and shiver. It's time.

The trees are all bare. We've already had the first snowfall. So into the basement goes my porch swing and with it disappears my prayer space. Time to prepare a new one inside.

I move my grandmother's old rocking chair into a prominent position in front of the picture window. I dig out the afghans my mother wove for me before she died. Let the winter try its worst.

Three generations of women are ready and waiting.

I give thanks to my God at every remembrance of you, praying always with joy in my every prayer for all of you, because of your partnership for the gospel from the first day until now. Phil 1:3-5

T.L.C.*

After days of being pampered during an illness, the child finally recovers. By this time, he or she has grown accustomed to large doses of T.L.C. Many simple tasks, like getting dressed and eating normal foods have been forgotten. Mom will do it.

The child tries to cling to his or her helplessness, even though Mom has exhausted her store of patience. The whines and moans that brought her running to see what's wrong just the other day, now evoke only irritation.

Mother's precious store of T.L.C. needs to be renewed and rebuilt.

*Tender Loving Care

When the wine ran short, the mother of Jesus said to him, "They have no wine." Jesus said to her, "Woman, how does your concern affect me? My hour has not yet come." His mother said to the servers, "Do whatever he tells you." Now there were six stone water jars there for Jewish ceremonial washings, each holding twenty to thirty gallons. Jesus told them, "Fill the jars with water." Jn 2:3-7

Not So Long Ago

Who is this mature young man walking properly up to receive that precious morsel of bread? I can remember him breaking loose from my grip not so long ago and running up and down the aisle during communion. I frantically chased after him while his dad frowned from the pew, holding his sister firmly in place.

It seemed, at the time, as though the experience would last forever. And, in some ways, it has.

For I received from the Lord what I also handed on to you, that the Lord Jesus, on the night he was handed over, took bread, and, after he had given thanks, broke it and said, "This is my body that is for you. Do this in remembrance of me." 1 Cor 11:23-24

> *Time Bandits*

There are these bandits who live in the corners of my life, and they steal my time. They consume it like video characters swallowing energy dots. Even while I sleep, they munch an hour here, a half hour there, so that I wake up already behind.

I haven't caught these bandits yet, but I hope they've got indigestion!

You have given my days a very short span; /my life is as nothing before you. /All mortals are but a breath. Ps 39:6

Not Alone

Some things are best done alone.

Mothering is not one of them.

May you experience the wisdom of this.

When you pass through the water, I will be with you; /in the rivers you shall not drown. /When you walk through fire, you shall not be burned; /the flames shall not consume you. /For I am the LORD, your God. Is 43:2-3

Video Generation

Video mania is attacking our young people. Like a computer virus, it's spreading throughout the system, erasing memories along the way.

There's video shopping, video aerobics, video movies, video games. Our children have no concept of a world without video. Everything comes to them through a TV screen.

How can mothers compete with this non-stop excitement and teach our children the value of sitting quietly by a stream?

Streams of the river gladden the city of God, /the holy dwelling of the Most High. Ps 46:5

Best Friends

My daughter and the neighbor girl are best friends. They simply have to see each other each day or they are in agony. They laugh together, they fight together, they cry together. They hug each other, reluctant to let go at the end of the day.

"Goodbye, best friend," they say, and kiss. I have to practically drag them apart to get my daughter in for the night.

Best friends. Life would be so awful without them.

A faithful friend is beyond price, /no sum can balance his worth. Sir 6:15

Lunch with the Girls

Lunch with the girls. My first chance since the baby's birth to get out by myself without children in tow. A chance to be free; to talk girl talk about men, make-up and clothing; to giggle, laugh, be with my friends.

I kiss my kids goodbye and leave them in the care of their aunt. A good time for them, a good time for me.

I rush to my car and race to the restaurant, hoping I'm not too late. Suddenly I realize I left my purse and took the diaper bag instead.

Lunch with the girls. Warm formula anyone?

But they said to him, "Five loaves and two fish are all we have here." Then he said, "Bring them here to me," and he ordered the crowds to sit down on the grass. Taking the five loaves and the two fish, and looking up to heaven, he said the blessing, broke the loaves, and gave them to the disciples, who in turn gave them to the crowds. Mt 14:17-19

Zookeeper

Just one cold rainy day and my children are already acting like caged animals. And it's not even winter yet!

Like animals, they prowl the house looking for trouble. The minute one kid is occupied, another one comes in and pinches, hits or aggravates until they end up rolling on the floor.

Then comes feeding time at the zoo. They make faces at each other, kick underneath the table, pick food from each other's plates, and try to hide food they don't want. I stand in the relative safety of the kitchen and toss food at them. With protective garb on and whip in hand, I approach them to remove the remainders of the meal from plate, table, chairs and wall. I then proceed to hose the room down.

Finally, with them safely locked down in their rooms for the night, I'm able to take off my zookeeper's uniform and relax from my constant vigilance.

Then I hear the roar every zookeeper dreads. "Mom, can I have a drink of water?"

At the time, all discipline seems a cause not for joy but for pain, yet later it brings the peaceful fruit of righteousness to those who are trained by it. So strengthen your drooping hands and your weak knees. Heb 12:11-12

> ### Goodbye

Hi, Mom. I'm here. I told you I would be. I promised so long ago. You were there for me when I first came into this world, and I want to be there for you when you leave it.

Please don't slip away without telling me first. Don't sneak away during the night when all the other residents of the nursing home are asleep. I want to be there, holding your hand. Don't try to spare me this loss. That would be harder than witnessing your journey from this world to the next.

I love you, Mom. You were the first voice I heard in this world, and I want mine to be the last you hear before starting your new life. Say "hi" to Dad for me. Tell him I love him too.

Goodbye, Mom. I'll remember you forever. I know you'll be watching me.

For she is the refulgence of eternal light, /the spotless mirror of the power of God, /the image of his goodness. Wis 7:26

White Bread and Canned Vegetables

My kids pass the germs they collect at school to each other and to me like candy at Halloween. We make an unending round of doctor visits for ear infections, bronchitis, strep throat, sinus infections. I don't remember being sick like this when I was a child. Visits to doctors' offices seemed extremely rare. There must be something wrong with my kids.

I pour over endless books on health and nutrition, pump my children with vitamins, fight with them daily over eating vegetables, buy brown bread over the less expensive and more popular white bread. Each day is a battle over their sugar intake.

And yet, despite my best efforts they get sick all the time.

I grew up on a diet of white bread, bologna sandwiches, hot dogs and canned vegetables. Maybe my mother knew something I don't.

For everything created by God is good, and nothing is to be rejected when received with thanksgiving, for it is made holy by the invocation of God in prayer. 1 Tm 4:4-5

Thanks

One of my greatest frustrations as a mother is the seeming ingratitude and demanding nature of my children. The more I give my kids, the more they want. What a blow when I realized that this is how I treat God—always wanting more, no matter how much I already have.

"That's nice, God. Now, if you could just take care of this other matter," I would pray.

So now I no longer pray for patience, I try to be patient. I no longer pray for joy, I try to be joyful. And I no longer pray for a thankful heart, I try to give thanks in all things, even during times when God seems distant.

I thank God for the good things I do have, confident that God loves me and will continue to provide for me and my family.

Enter the temple gates with praise, /its courts with thanksgiving. /Give thanks to God, bless his name; /good indeed is the Lord, /Whose love endures forever, /whose faithfulness lasts through every age. Ps 100:4-5

> **Boundaries**

Mothers are finite. Like all of creation, we have a beginning and an end. Those are the concrete boundaries that frame us. There's no escaping them.

This is good for our children. Every child needs to be able to recognize that here is where Mom ends, there is where child begins.

Mothers also need to know that we are not our children, our children are not us. We are separate entities.

Yet it is important for both mothers and children to understand that there is something that recognizes no boundaries—a powerful force that binds us together at the core of our being.

That force is love, which is another name for God.

[Love] bears all things, believes all things, hopes all things, endures all things. Love never fails. 1 Cor 13:7-8

> *Grandmother's House*

I'm going home for the holidays. Pack the kids. Pack the bags. Pack the car and off we go. Put aside the job. Put aside the household chores. Put aside all the worries of the day. They'll wait. I'm going home.

Time to be pampered. Time for catching up on all the news; for food and fun. No troubles. No worries. Just time to be with family and friends.

The kids are so excited. They are going to Grandmother's house.

Over the river and through the woods . . . .

During those days Mary set out and traveled to the hill country in haste to a town of Judah, where she entered the house of Zechariah and greeted Elizabeth. Lk 1:39-40

Indulge Now

'Tis the season to indulge

Fa la la la la, la la la la.

Today we eat, tomorrow we bulge,

Fa la la la la, la la la la.

Blow up like a parade balloon,

Fa la la, la la la, la la la.

Then we'll hibernate 'til June,

Fa la la la la, la la la la.

---

*The LORD of hosts /will provide for all peoples
/A feast of rich food and choice wines, /juicy,
rich food and pure, choice wines. Is 25:6*

One Day of Domesticity

One year of domesticity crammed into one day. This is the day she cleans the house, bakes bread and pies, makes cookies with her children, reads them bedtime stories and then collapses into bed while they stay up watching TV.

She wants to give her children the memory of their mother with flour on her nose and arms covered with bread dough. She wants them to have the same memories she has of her mother.

Who is she kidding? Her mother didn't work outside the home. Can she really expect her children to remember her in an apron? They'll remember their mom coming home exhausted from work, slipping off her shoes and collapsing after popping frozen dinners in the microwave.

But they'll love her anyway.

"Whoever humbles himself like this child is the greatest in the kingdom of heaven. And whoever receives one child such as this in my name receives me." Mt 18:4-5

More of the Same

I'm forty years old today and I have everything I thought I ever wanted in this world. I have a home, husband, children, meaningful employment. What else is there in life?

I've spent most of my life striving to reach this point, but what is left for me? I feel so old. Before I know it, I'll be sitting in my rocking chair waiting for my grandchildren to visit. Oh, God, my life is half over. What will the next half hold for me?

If I'm lucky, more of the same.

You have been born anew, not from perishable but from imperishable seed, through the living and abiding word of God, for: "All flesh is like grass, /and all its glory like the flower of the field; /the grass withers, /and the flower wilts; /but the word of the Lord remains forever."
1 Pt 1:23-25

The Right to Grieve

They say I can have other children. That I'm young. That I'll forget the pain of these days when I finally hold a child in my arms. Their words seem shallow, meaningless.

They don't know the emptiness I feel. The death of hope. The death of promise. The small life that was all potential waiting to be realized never got a chance. All my dreams for the future, dashed in a rush of blood. That small quickening life gone for good.

Some people say it wasn't even a baby—just a fetus. But I knew from the moment I felt that life move that my baby was a person-in-the-making.

So don't deny me the right to grieve. Don't deny this child or my loss. I'll get over it, but I won't forget.

From my loud groaning /I became just skin and bones. /I am like a desert owl, /like an owl among the ruins. /I lie awake and moan, /like a lone sparrow on the roof. Ps 102:6-8

Farther Along

"Farther along we'll know all about it. Farther along we'll understand why." The gospel song tells us this and we believe in its truth. There's so much in this world we mothers can't comprehend: children with disabilities, children who disappoint, children who die. Our hope is in the next life, where we will confront God face to face. Then we will understand all that we don't understand now. Or will we?

Perhaps understanding is just another invention of our rational minds. We continue to chase after the illusion of understanding and, if we can't understand now, then we hold on to the hope of understanding in the next world. But some things we can't understand. It takes faith to go on in the face of so much darkness.

Maybe it doesn't really matter whether we understand or not. We know that we will see God someday and be happy with God forever. That's enough to know.

Though I tried to understand all this, /it was too difficult for me, /Till I entered the sanctuary of God /and came to understand. Ps 73:16-17

December 1

Sleeping Children

There's nothing quite like sleeping children. There's an aura about them that's almost unreal. That these bundles of energy can finally come to a halt doesn't seem possible. That their mouths should ever be silent is almost unnerving. We see sleeping children in a whole new light. No more screaming, no more commotion, only peace.

I push a path to their beds through toys and clothes, brush the hair out of their eyes, and cover them with blankets before implanting kisses on their foreheads. What only moments ago were chatterboxes in the eternal battle over bedtime are now silent. The quiet is rich. It's a pregnant silence, broken only by slight rising and lowering of their little chests.

I remove a toy gun from my son's arms and replace it with a teddy.

The cow and the bear shall be neighbors, /together their young shall rest; /the lion shall eat hay like the ox. Is 11:7

God's Pretty Lights

Each morning I delight in looking out the window at the sunrise. They're God's pretty lights, I tell my children.

"Come on, let's go see if God has turned on the pretty lights yet," I tell my children when they get up early. This brings me a little more quiet time while we all gaze out the window for glimpses of pink.

God's pretty lights are far better than any manufactured ones I've ever seen. So much more beautiful because we can't just turn them off and on at will, but can only catch them when God chooses.

God. Nobody does it better.

Great are the works of the LORD, /to be treasured for all their delights. Ps 111:2

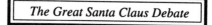

The Great Santa Claus Debate

The great Santa Claus debate goes on. Do we let children believe in Santa or not? Regardless of what we tell them, they will believe what they want. Isn't that so? What's the harm in a little Christmas magic?

But then what happens when Mom and Dad can't come through with the expensive gifts the kids expect from Santa? And what happens to their trust in adults when they are finally told the truth?

I worry over these questions, then give in to the culture around me. Who am I to fight society? It wants us to believe in Santa and spends enormous amounts of money and energy to perpetuate this belief.

If only society felt as strongly about God.

Give me neither poverty nor riches; /provide me only with the food I need; /Lest, being full, I deny you, /saying, "Who is the Lord?"
Prv 30:8-9

Long Has She Waited

How long she has waited for this child! Not nine months, but nine years. Nine years of trying, of being disappointed. Nine years of longing, of trips to fertility specialists, and finally of visits to social workers and reams of adoption applications—all to make ready for this long-awaited day. Nine years of waiting to win the title "mother."

They place the baby in her arms. She's nervous, and fearful, and excited. She doesn't want to hear about the heartaches to come, the special joy and pain of adoption, the child's struggle for identity. She just wants to hold and love her baby.

No one will ever say this child was unwanted. No child could have been wanted more.

---

*I prayed for this child, and the L*ORD* granted my request. 1 Sam 1:27*

Enough Is Enough

Enough just isn't enough anymore. That seems to be the message we get, especially during the holiday season. No matter what we have, we want more. We want bigger and better cars and houses and presents and celebrations. We pile up accomplishments or degrees, but none of these things satisfy our need.

We constantly take on more responsibilities, more activities, more debt. We've lost the ability to know when we've had enough. Nothing fills the emptiness that lies within.

It's only when we face that emptiness that we can be filled. It's only when we know our own inadequacies and failures that we can realize how totally lovable we are to God.

God completes our lack, heals our brokenness, and makes us whole. Without God, nothing we do is enough. With God, enough is enough.

For by grace you have been saved through faith, and this is not from you; it is the gift of God; it is not from works, so no one may boast. For we are his handiwork, created in Christ Jesus for the good works that God has prepared in advance, that we should live in them.
Eph 2:8-10

Promises

Promises left unfulfilled—they haunt me in the middle of the night, when I am powerless to do anything about them. By morning, they are swept away by the many duties of the day. The ambitions of a young girl were overcome by the realities of motherhood and the daily demands of everyday life.

Whatever happened to that young girl and the promises she made to herself? She would never become like her own mother—old and staid, never having lived beyond the four walls of her home. She would have a life of adventure. Children would fit into that life too. She'd take them with her backpacking in the Smoky Mountains, white water rafting, traveling the Alaskan highway.

Are promises any less important because they were made to yourself? Can they be broken because no one knew about them but you?

When God made the promise to Abraham, since he had no one greater by whom to swear, "he swore by himself." Heb 6:13

Witch Children

It stands to reason that witch moms would produce witch children. My children have days when my slightest word or look elicits a snarl. They are best left alone to work it out. After all, they haven't perfected their witchiness yet. Who knows what damage they may do while exercising their young powers?

We all—male or female, child or adult—need to be witchy at times. If we mothers can show our children we love them even on their bad days, if we can show love for the dark side as well as the good sides of their personalities, we go a long way towards teaching them to love themselves.

That is the surest cure for witchery.

It may be that God will grant them repentance that leads to knowledge of the truth, and that they may return to their senses out of the devil's snare. 2 Tm 2:25-26

The Faithful Ones

In a faithless world, some women shine forth as faithful to a faith not their own, to people who are no blood relation to them. There are thousands of Ruths in this world.

They faithfully tend the dying as nurses, health care workers, or just friends. They teach our children in schools and pass on our faith at Sunday School. Their caring reaches far beyond their own families.

For this they receive little recognition, few monetary rewards, rare notices in the paper. But they do receive the love of those they serve and fidelity in return. Faithfulness builds faithfulness.

Children, let us love not in word or speech but in deed and truth. 1 Jn 3:18

Someday

"Mommy, someday can we go to Mickey Mouse World?" my four-year-old asks plaintively.

"Someday, maybe someday," I reply with resignation. Someday when nothing is broken and in need of repair or replacement. Someday when your dad can take time from work. Someday when the kids aren't all in school. Someday.

My life is full of somedays. Sometimes someday arrives, other times it never appears. Someday we'll paint the house. Someday I'll plant that garden. Someday we'll visit Europe. Someday we'll buy a dishwasher. Too many things are put off till someday. Sometimes, if you ignore something enough, it just goes away. Sometimes the urgency fades until the desire disappears altogether.

Maybe someday we'll go to Mickey Mouse world. But if we put it off indefinitely, someday may never come.

That would be a shame.

For you yourselves know very well that the day of the Lord will come like a thief in the night.
1 Thes 5:2

> *Working Mother's Guilt*

The note is slipped into my hand: Call your son's school. What is it now? Is he sick? In trouble?

He was in a fight on the playground and has a broken nose. They are taking him to the emergency room. Yes, I'll meet them there.

Why does he do this to me constantly? He knows I'm busy. I leave a message on my husband's beeper and head for the hospital.

Yet another crisis at school. Yet another case of working mother's guilt. Each crisis in my children's lives creates a crisis in my professional life as I grapple with balancing career and motherhood. Why can't I do both?

Working mother's guilt—is there ever an end to it?

"No one can serve two masters." Mt. 6:24

Gifts

Do you know any morose, unhappy people? The bank teller who grouches at the customers or the snippy salesclerk? Maybe they are this way because they have gifts that have never been used, dreams that have not been realized. Maybe they've spent their lives living out other people's expectations, until they have become too tired to do something about their own.

Kids pick up immediately on such people. "Mom, why is that man so crabby?" "Mom, what's the matter with her?"

It's up to us mothers to point out the tragedy of a life not lived to its potential, of gifts never used. We also need to teach our kids that it's never too late to begin.

So, the next time you encounter that grouchy bankteller or snippy salesclerk, smile at him or her and say hello. There might still be a dream waiting to be realized.

Your children will be watching.

Rid yourselves of all malice and all deceit, insincerity, envy, and all slander; like newborn infants, long for pure spiritual milk so that through it you may grow into salvation, for you have tasted that the Lord is good. 1 Pt 2:1-3

Roses in December

Mary, Jesus' mother, gave Juan Diego of Guadalupe roses in December as proof for a doubting bishop of her existence—or so the story goes. Mary offers all mothers roses in December—gifts of hope during the dark times, the times of trial and suffering. We've only to stop and notice them. They are there, present for all of us with eyes of faith.

Roses in December. God's mother is with every mother, always.

"Have you come to believe because you have seen me? Blessed are those who have not seen and have believed." Jn 20:29

> *Therapy*

Life with kids is not fair. They can fight and throw tantrums, but the minute I yell, I'm the bad guy. Everything is somehow my fault. Mom is supposed to rise above every battle with a calm, loving, patient demeanor.

Twenty years from now my kids will all be in therapy, telling their therapist what a terrible mother I was.

In the meantime, I'm looking for a therapist to listen to me.

I will instruct you and show you the way you should walk, /give you counsel and watch over you. Ps 32:8

> *Rome Wasn't Built In a Day*

Children have so little patience. It's hard for them to comprehend what it is like to work for hours, day after day, to build something. Anything that takes more than fifteen minutes is a monumental task of such proportion that it boggles their little minds.

Maybe patience is all in your mind—a matter of time perspective.

Sure Rome wasn't built in a day. But it was built by adults. Pre-schoolers would have finished it in two hours, if that long.

But as for the seed that fell on rich soil, they are the ones who, when they have heard the word, embrace it with a generous and good heart, and bear fruit through perserverance. Lk 8:15

It seems that everybody who has anything to do with children wants to have a Christmas celebration of some sort, leaving me feeling very Scrooge-like as I try to deal with children bouncing off the wall from the sweets that keep appearing in their hands. It's very hard to experience the peace of Christ amidst all of this. Even the most patient of mothers exhibits a tense smile as her children receive yet another Christmas goody accompanied by phrases like "Christmas only comes once a year," and "What will one little cookie hurt?"

All these well-wishers who want to do something special for my children at this time deprive me of much of the joy of doing the extras myself. My time is spent trying to counteract my kids' overexcitement, rather than adding to it.

Part of me waits in anticipation for Christmas, but part of me dreads the day. No amount of preparation on my part can possibly match the elaborate expectations my children have.

Hope does not disappoint, because the love of God has been poured out into our hearts through the holy Spirit that has been given to us.
Rom 5:5

Charity

Here comes another charity group bearing gifts. For this they expect her to be thankful. Thankful for being humiliated in the eyes of her children because she is unable to provide for them in the manner these do-gooders deem appropriate.

She holds her head high and takes all that is given as her rightful due. Underneath her politeness, she hates the givers for her dependence.

This year, Lord, she prays, give me what I need—not what they choose to give.

So humble yourselves under the mighty hand of God, that he may exalt you in due time. Cast all your worries upon him because he cares for you. 1 Pt 5:6-7

Abandoned

The car pulls up. An elderly woman is helped out, put into a wheelchair and pushed through the emergency room door. The car drives away and never returns. Pinned to the woman's blouse is the note: Please take care of me.

That's all. No name, no mention of family, no medical records. Abandoned like a newborn babe on a doorstep.

The woman looks confused and can't answer the simplest questions. The medical staff doesn't know what to do with her. She's come back to die in the place where her babies were born.

Then the LORD asked Cain, "Where is your brother Abel" He answered, "I do not know. Am I my brother's keeper?" Gn 4:9

What Will the Neighbors Say?

One thing that I vowed never to say to my children is "what will the neighbors say?" That phrase echoed through my ears too many times as a child.

Now, I've made many vows that I later broke, but this one I've kept. With gritted teeth I've watched my children parade off to school in clashing outfits they selected themselves. I've allowed them to wear their "favorite" clothes long past the time they should have been passed to the rag bag or to someone smaller. I've mentally heard all the negative neighborly comments about how my children look and have still managed to refrain from squelching their expressions of self.

Bravely have I walked through many a public place with screaming children in tow, assuring myself that other mothers have been through the same thing and understand. I remind myself constantly that my children need the freedom to be individuals. They aren't just reflections of, and on, me.

So I choose not to worry what the neighbors might say or to concern myself about the gossips' tongues. After all, if Mary had worried about what the neighbors would say, she may not have had Jesus.

---

*When his mother Mary was betrothed to
Joseph, but before they lived together, she was
found with child through the holy Spirit. Mt :18*

```
┌──────────────┐
│  Oooops!     │
└──────────────┘
```

The test came back today. She had delayed learning the truth as long as she possibly could.

Oooops! After all of the baby clothes had been given away, after the high chair and crib were packed away in anticipation of future grandchildren, after looking forward to her new freedom when her last child would be in school—comes this unexpected news. Pregnant at forty-three! More years of broken sleep to come. Two more years (at least!) of spit-up and dirty diapers.

How will her husband react? He's just started to enjoy being a dad. How will her other kids take this? Giving up their room space, adjusting their habits and needs to the presence of a new baby, sharing the attention with one more personality.

How will she herself take the news?

She laughs in delight.

———————————

But the LORD said to Abraham: "Why did Sarah laugh and say, 'Shall I really bear a child, old as I am?' Is anything too marvelous for the LORD to do?" Gn 18:13-14

Boxes

If relationships were boxes,
we could tie them with a bow.
We could gift wrap them with paper
and line them in a row.

Here would be our children,
center place our spouse.
Friends, extended family would be
sprinkled 'round the house.

But relationships aren't boxes
sitting neatly in their place.
They bump and bruise each other
and invade each other's space.

"Do you think that I have come to establish peace on the earth? No, I tell you, but rather division." Lk 12:51

| The Beginner's Slope |

We trudge together, my children and I, to the hill on the back forty, sleds in tow. What a wonderful way to spend a winter day.

The kids laugh with glee at bumps and mishaps, pouting at aborted trips when they get so far and stop. They quickly abandon the small "beginner" hills with smooth, even rides for the higher, more treacherous slopes. They aim for the rough spots, laughing when they spill.

If only I could glide over the rough places in my life like these children on their sleds. I would pick myself up after each tumble and hurry back up the hill in anticipation of the next ride.

But I'm still on the beginner's slope of life.

We are afflicted in every way, but not constrained; perplexed, but not driven to despair; persecuted, but not abandoned; struck down, but not destroyed. 2 Cor 4:8-9

Home Alone

Not every home is a good place to be over the holidays. Some homes are broken beyond repair.

Her children are with her husband for the week. Her own parents are dead, her in-laws are no longer hers. Her friends are busy with their own families.

She has no place to go, no one to share her feelings with.

She is home alone for Christmas.

———————————————

God is faithful, and by him you were called to fellowship. 1 Cor 1:9

White Christmas

She's not dreaming of a white Christmas. She's enjoying the green and the warmth. Whence comes the illusion that the best Christmas is a white Christmas? Give her sun and fun and surf! She'll lounge by the pool and listen to Christmas music, thank you.

At least one half of the world never has snow at Christmas. Are they somehow inferior? Doomed to a less meaningful existence? Who decreed that Christmases were meant to be spent huddled indoors around a roaring fire rather than spent in a bathing suit on a beach next to the ocean?

For her, the most important thing is that she'll be with her kids at Christmas.

Pass the suntan lotion, please.

"Look about you, and from where you are, gaze to the north and south, east and west; all the land that you see I will give to you and your descendents. Gn 13:14-15

Extremes

The holiday season is a time of extremes: extreme hope, extreme despair; extreme expectations, extreme disappointments. TV sets us up for these extremes. Happy families gathered around the table with piles of presents and good cheer are juxtaposed with stories of heartache, loss, and depression.

What I'd like is a holiday that is average: no big hoopla, no big to-do, just—you know—average. A truly peaceful Christmas without a lot of commotion, wound-up children, and disappointed in-laws.

Wasn't that how the first Christmas was? Just a simple birth of a child. A normal, ordinary event.

Yet miraculous, in the extreme.

"Glory to God in the highest /and on earth peace to those on whom his favor rests."
Lk 2:14

> *Merry Christmas*

In a sense, every time a baby is born it is Christmas. Within each child lies a promise yet to be fulfilled.

It is the job of the mother to nurture that promise to fulfillment.

Within each Christmas lies the potential of Easter.

---

*For a child is born to us, a son is given us;
/upon his shoulder dominion rests. /They name
him Wonder-Counselor, God-Hero, /Father-
Forever, Prince of Peace. Is 9:5*

Battle of the Bulge

I gained thirty pounds overnight! Fat cells crept under the covers and attacked me while I slept. Why me and not my husband? Why is he immune to the creeping fatties?

Put on the sweatsuit, get out the exercise bike, run ten miles before daylight. Grapefruit for breakfast, carrot sticks for lunch, throw out all those holiday munchies . . .

Here I stand, another casualty in the battle of the bulge.

Every athlete exercises discipline in every way.
They do it to win a perishable crown, but we an
imperishable one. 1 Cor 9:25

All By Name

My daughter's room is filled with her babies—dolls and stuffed animals she can't live without. She knows them all by name. Each year, with the arrival of new babies at Christmas, I encourage her to get rid of the old ones that are falling apart. No luck.

The one time I did manage to get rid of one of her stuffed animals remains vivid in my memory. It was a rabbit picked up for a quarter at a garage sale. Normal wear and tear led to a missing paw with a wire protruding. Not a safe toy, so I put it on top of the refrigerator assuring her that "Daddy will fix it."

After what I felt was a sufficient passage of time, the rabbit went into the wastebasket. Then I heard, "Mommy, when is Daddy going to fix my bunny. I love that old thing."

"When he gets time," I told her. Months pass. Christmas came and went, bringing new babies. Still she asked about her bunny. I told her that Santa took it to his workshop to fix. The next Christmas arrived.

"Mommy, Santa forgot to bring Bunny back to me. I love that old thing."

Never again will I throw out a toy with a name.

———————————

Fear not, for I have redeemed you; /I have called you by name: you are mine. Is 43:1

Coming into My Own

People whom I thought were my age suddenly are much older. They got gray overnight. Or did I just now notice the balding heads and pot bellies?

I, on the other hand, have gotten younger with the years. Now that I've lived to see my children successfully raised, I'm coming into my own!

Now there was a man in Jerusalem whose name was Simeon. This man was righteous and devout, awaiting the consolation of Israel, and the holy Spirit was upon him. It had been revealed to him by the holy Spirit that he should not see death before he had seen the Messiah of the Lord Lk 2:25-26

> *Motherland*

"Curiouser and curiouser," said Alice in Wonderland. I might say the same about Motherland: topsy, turvy; upside-down, inside-out; dead-ends; running in circles, chasing my tail.

Let your mother and father have joy; /let her who bore you exult. Prv 23:25

Corpse

Lord, have mercy on me. The wrapping paper is hardly off the presents and already I'm inundated with the bills. It kind of takes some of the glow off Christmas!

The tax man has no mercy either. This year isn't even cold in its grave yet and out come the tax forms. What a cruel reminder of year's end.

Couldn't we just once have a nice clean burial of the past year without carrying the corpse into the next?

Pay to all their dues, taxes to whom taxes are due, toll to whom toll is due, respect to whom respect is due, honor to whom honor is due. Rom 13:7

> *Love*

So ends another year. Dreams fulfilled, opportunities missed. Heartaches mixed with joy. Time to let all of that go. Let it sink into the forgiving glow of memory.

Hold on only to love, mother, and it will multiply in abundance, overflowing and spilling forth into next year and the years to come.

―――――――――――――――

"I have told you this so that my joy might be in you and your joy might be complete. This is my commandment: love one another as I love you."
Jn 15:11-12